TIM FLANNERY

EXPLORING THE MOST MYSTERIOUS LEVELS OF THE OCEAN

DEEP DIVE INTO DEEP SEA

ILLUSTRATED BY
SAM CALDWELL

Text copyright © 2020 by Tim Flannery
Illustrations copyright © 2020 by Sam Caldwell
Design copyright © 2020 by Hardie Grant Egmont
Research by Emma Flannery
First American Edition 2022

First published in Australia by Hardie Grant Children's Publishing as
EXPLORE YOUR WORLD: Deep Dive into Deep Sea

For information about permission to reproduce selections from this book, write to
Permissions, W. W. Norton & Company, Inc., 500 Fifth Avenue, New York, NY 10110

For information about special discounts for bulk purchases, please contact
W. W. Norton Special Sales at specialsales@wwnorton.com or 800-233-4830

Manufacturing by TransContinental
Production manager: Julia Druskin
Internal design by Kristy Lund-White

Library of Congress Cataloging-in-Publication Data

Names: Flannery, Tim F. (Tim Fridtjof), 1956– author. | Caldwell, Sam (Illustrator), illustrator.
Title: Deep dive into deep sea : exploring the most mysterious levels of the ocean /
Tim Flannery ; art by Sam Caldwell.
Description: First American Edition. | New York : Norton Young Readers, [2022] |
Series: Explore your world | "Exploring the Most Mysterious Levels of the Ocean"—
Cover page 1. | Audience: Ages 9–12 years
Identifiers: LCCN 2021050493 | ISBN 9781324019770 (Hardcover) | ISBN 9781324019787 (ePub)
Subjects: LCSH: Ocean—Juvenile literature | Marine animals—Juvenile literature. |
Fishes—Juvenile literature.
Classification: LCC GC21.5 .F569 2022 | DDC 577.7—dc23/eng/20211203
LC record available at https://lccn.loc.gov/2021050493

W. W. Norton & Company, Inc., 500 Fifth Avenue, New York, N.Y. 10110
www.wwnorton.com

W. W. Norton & Company Ltd., 15 Carlisle Street, London W1D 3BS

2 4 6 8 0 9 7 5 3 1

TIM FLANNERY

EXPLORING THE MOST MYSTERIOUS LEVELS OF THE OCEAN

DEEP DIVE INTO DEEP SEA

ILLUSTRATED BY SAM CALDWELL

Norton Young Readers

An Imprint of W. W. Norton & Company
Independent Publishers Since 1923

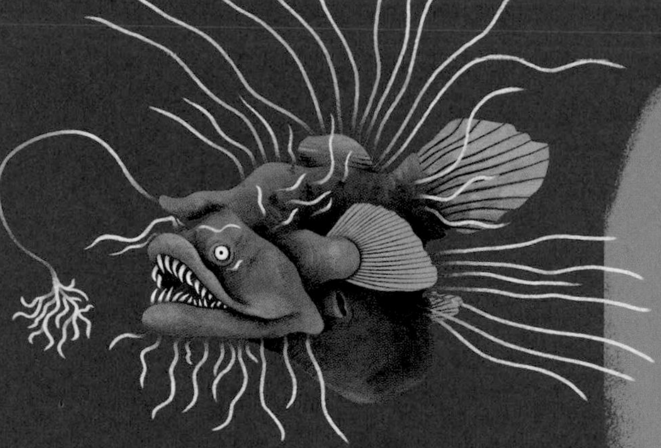

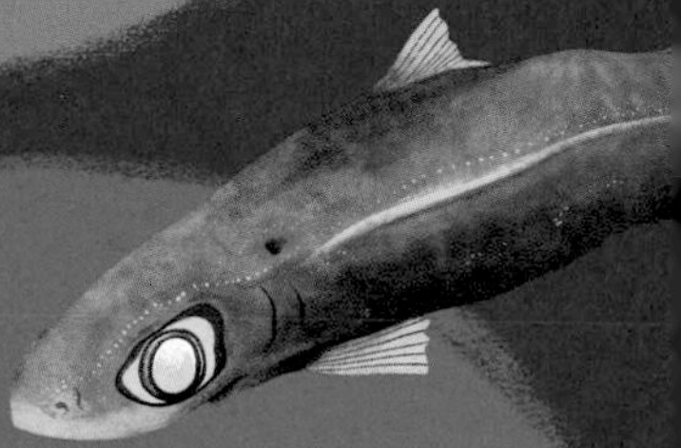

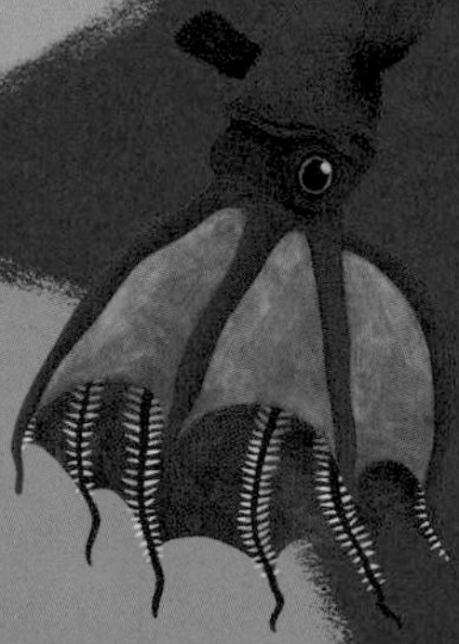

INTRODUCTION

I have always loved the ocean. I used to scuba dive, and the deepest I ever got was almost 100 feet when I was 16 years old. We dived into a shipping channel in Port Phillip Bay, Australia—which you would not be allowed to do today! I remember the immense blackness. I wasn't able to see anything, and there was no clearly defined bottom, just a dark ooze that got slightly thicker the deeper you sank into it. I wasn't even sure which way was up, so I took my mouthpiece out and blew some bubbles and they went sideways! I was lying on my side when I thought I was standing up!

The ocean deep—which is much, much farther down than that—is even harder for humans to deal with. Yet there are many creatures that live in those parts of the ocean, and this book will introduce you to them.

The ocean deep is bewildering and remarkable. It can be incredibly beautiful, as well as truly terrifying. The conditions here are extreme. Imagine you have ventured down into this mysterious and remote place. First, you feel entirely lost in the penetrating pitch-black. Every direction you turn feels like an endless black dream. Next, you notice the ice-cold water. You are submerged in close to freezing temperatures—goosebumps are the least of your worries! Lastly, you begin to feel awfully uncomfortable: as the intense water pressure builds, it squashes every part of your body.

This does not seem like the most welcoming of environments, and you may be wondering how any animal can survive down there. The answer is with the most unusual and fascinating adaptations to suit their home, from incredible eyesight to inventive ways to trap and eat food. Some creatures have bodies with flashing lights, or fishing rods coming out of their heads, an expandable stomach or eyes the size of your head. You might find it hard to believe that some of the creatures in this book are real, but I assure you they certainly are!

THE DEEPEST PART OF THE OCEAN MAKES UP NiNE-TENTHS OF ALL HABiTAT ON EARTH.

But it remains largely a mystery; we really don't know much about it. We know more about the surface of the moon than we do about the deepest parts of the ocean. Twelve people have walked on the moon, but only four have descended below 20,000 feet—and that's only halfway to the bottom of the ocean! We should know more about this fascinating part of the world, and this is where

I hope this book helps. For example, do you know the names of the planets? Some of the constellations? Now, try to name one of the deepest parts of the ocean and see how you do. There's so much to explore deep below the ocean and we only know a fraction of it!

There are a few reasons for that. First, it's really hard to get there. For most of us, a snorkel only works to about 30 feet, while free divers (those who dive with no equipment) can travel down to 300 feet. Very special scuba (self-contained underwater breathing apparatus) equipment can help us dive around 1,000 feet, but after that the immense pressure means the human body just can't survive. Submarines can travel even farther, but still not deep enough to see a deep-sea creature. Second, deep-sea exploration equipment is very expensive so not everyone has access to it.

The extreme pressure you would feel at the bottom of the ocean is unlike anything you would have experienced before. Our atmosphere is

made up of all the gases that surround Earth and, although it doesn't feel like it, we feel some pressure from our atmosphere on the surface of our planet. But in the ocean deep there is much more. With every 30 feet of water the pressure is increased by one of our surface atmospheres. So the entire atmosphere of our planet applies as much pressure as just the top 30 feet of the ocean! At the very deepest part of the sea, 7 miles down, the pressure is the equivalent of a full-sized male African elephant, weighing 15,000 pounds, standing on the end of your big toe!

OUCH!

THE BODIES OF ALL ANIMALS AND PLANTS ARE MADE UP OF TINY BUILDING BLOCKS CALLED MOLECULES.

Molecules are at risk of being crushed when under pressure. That's why humans need special underwater vessels to protect themselves when they visit the deep ocean.

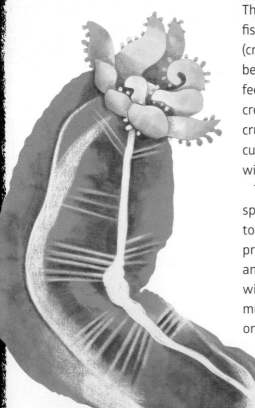

But deep-sea creatures have found a way to protect themselves from this pressure. They have a special type of molecule called **piezolytes** that protect them from getting crushed in the depths. We know that deep-sea creatures must smell "fishy," because piezolytes have a fishy smell, and deep-sea creatures have lots of them! Even the tiniest of tiny creatures that live at the bottom of the ocean, the ones you can only see under a microscope, use piezolytes to protect themselves. But below a certain depth even piezolytes can't protect fish. That is why there are no fish, or other vertebrates (creatures with a backbone), below around 30,000 feet deep. Some types of creatures, like specialized crustaceans and sea cucumbers, somehow cope with the intense pressure.

The animals of the deep spend all of their lives trying to find a meal, avoiding predators, and finding another creature to mate with. But they don't need much food. Fish living a mile or more down require only a hundredth as much energy as those on the surface. Due to the severe cold, all of the processes in their body are so slowed down that, to us more active beings, they seem to be almost suspended between life and death. This can also mean some animals down there can live for a very long time. You will meet one of the longest-lived animals on Earth in this book—the deep-sea coral (page 96).

The deep ocean may seem so far away that it is not affected by how we live at the surface. But climate change is beginning to reach even its deepest parts, with scientists observing an increase in water temperatures.

OCEAN CURRENTS ARE VERY IMPORTANT IN BRINGING OXYGEN TO THE OCEAN DEEP, AND AS OUR CLIMATE CHANGES THEY MAY BE AFFECTED.

But one of the biggest pollution problems facing the deep today is garbage. Plastic waste has been found even at the deepest part of the ocean, and some of the creatures down there have been eating plastic. We don't yet know what effect it has on them, but think about it next time you see plastic on the street or beach. You might be doing a deep-sea creature a great favor by putting that plastic in a trash can.

If you are interested in the deep sea, there are several aquariums and research institutes around the world that have websites and video channels that can give you a first-hand glimpse at life in the deep. Also, when you are at the beach, watch out for things that get washed to shore and check in with your local museum if you think it is interesting! Often that's how scientists find out more and more about these fascinating creatures.

HAVE FUN!

When I was very young I often wished that I had a book that would tell me all about the mysteries of the deep. That's what I have tried to create here for you! Hopefully, in your lifetime more secrets of the deep will reveal themselves to scientists and we'll learn a lot more about these weird and amazing creatures that make our planet special. Or perhaps it just might be **you** who discovers a new deep-sea animal! *Tim Flannery*

A NOTE ON SCIENTIFIC NAMES

Not every creature has a common name, but every creature that has been classified has a scientific name. A scientific name helps scientists keep track of every new animal or plant on Earth. It also helps them understand how the new organism is related to all other life. A scientific name is made up of a genus and a species name. For example, for the deepest fish ever found, **Abyssobrotula** is the genus name and **galatheae** is the species name. Scientists like to write these names in italics to show they are the scientific name of the organism. Sometimes these names can be very long and confusing! To save scientists from writing out these long names every time, they often shorten the genus name to its first letter, for example, **A. galatheae**.

THE OCEAN'S ZONES

Over 70 percent of the world's surface is covered in water, and more than 95 percent of that water is in our salty oceans. That's a lot of water for many different fascinating creatures to live in! Spanning the Earth is one huge global ocean. Humans have divided this global ocean into five large bodies of water, each with a geographic boundary and its own name. These five names are: the Atlantic Ocean, the Pacific Ocean, the Indian Ocean, the Arctic Ocean and the Southern Ocean. There are also more than 50 seas on our globe. A sea is smaller than an ocean and is always bordering land. Some seas that you may have heard of include the Mediterranean Sea, the Caribbean Sea and the Tasman Sea.

The water on the world's surface doesn't only change from east to west as you move around the globe—it also changes from top to bottom. The average depth of the ocean is 12,000 feet, but in some parts of the world it can reach depths of almost 36,000 feet! The very top of the ocean is a completely different place than the very bottom. As you dive deeper, it becomes darker, colder and more highly pressurized. The ocean is divided up into five zones, and each one forms its own distinct habitat.

THE SUNLIT ZONE

This is the part of the ocean where seaweed can flourish and familiar fish and other sea creatures abound. It is the zone we can visit and study most easily, and the one we know most about. The water can be tropical warm or Arctic frigid. But the one thing that's always there, during the daytime at least, is sunlight. On average, the Sunlit Zone extends down just 650 feet. This book delves into the more mysterious ocean zones—those that are deep down below and much harder to reach.

THE TWILIGHT ZONE

Ninety percent of all the ocean's water lies below 650 feet, and its volume is 11 times greater than the area of all of the land above the sea. The Twilight Zone extends from 650 feet to 3,300 feet and lies just beyond the reach of most sunlight, with less than 1 percent remaining. Even though there is little sunlight, there is still a lot of light down there. That is because many Twilight Zone creatures produce their own light.

THE MIDNIGHT ZONE

Below the Twilight Zone lies the Midnight Zone, which extends from 3,300 feet to 9,900 feet. The water there is very cold—just 40 degrees Fahrenheit—and no light reaches it so no plants can grow. All inhabitants of the Midnight Zone are either scavengers (which means they eat things that are already dead) or predators. Even modern military submarines cannot enter the Midnight Zone—the water pressure is just too great.

— HYDROTHERMAL VENTS —

You might imagine that the Earth is one big, solid rock beneath your feet, motionless and unchanging. But the truth is that the Earth is made up of four main layers, each containing different minerals. Some of them are even moving! In the very middle is the dense core, followed by an outer core, then the mantle—which is mostly made of molten rock—and finally the thin crust on top. The mantle is very hot, ranging from 7,200 degrees Fahrenheit at its deepest point to 400 degrees Fahrenheit where it meets the crust. The crust is what you are standing on right now, but there is also crust deep in the ocean. In the very middle of the ocean, oceanic crust is being torn apart and new crust is being formed. This is one of the most astonishing habitats. Here, hot rocks from the Earth's mantle come close to the ocean floor, and superheated sea water rich in minerals escapes from cracks in rocks and flows into the sea. These are called hydrothermal vents, and are used by creatures that are entirely independent of energy from the sun. These vents support lots of unusual life—the number of creatures around the vents is 10,000 to 100,000 times more than on the surrounding ocean floor. Worms 6 feet long, great hosts of shrimps, and clams as long as your forearm dominate these ecosystems.

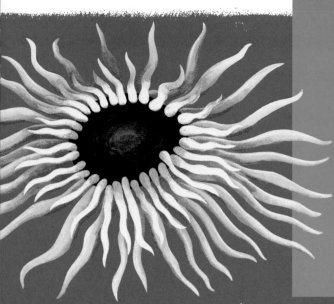

THE ABYSS

The Abyss lies below the Midnight Zone. It extends from 9,900 to 19,700 feet and its name means "bottomless" in Greek. It is not the bottom of the ocean though, for deep-sea trenches extend even deeper. The Abyssal Zone makes up over 80 percent of the ocean and covers 60 percent of the Earth. Temperatures are just above 32 degrees Fahrenheit.

WHALE AND SHIP FALLS

Dead whales and sunken ships make up another distinct habitat in the ocean deep. Whales that die and fall into the ocean deep are known as whale fall. They can feed entire ecosystems for decades. In fact, some creatures are only found on or around whale carcasses. Ships also sink, and there are about 3 million shipwrecks littering the ocean floor. It is estimated that a ship was lost at sea every two days between 1971 and 1990. Just like whales, they can support life in the Abyss. But the types of creatures living off a ship are different to those that live off dead whales.

THE TRENCHES

The deepest parts of the ocean are the Trenches. They are long furrows found in all oceans, and the deepest is the Mariana Trench. The Challenger Deep, its deepest part, lies 35,850 feet below the surface. In ocean trenches water pressure can be 1,000 times greater than at the surface, the temperature is near freezing, and it's pitch-black. Very few things live in the deep trenches—it's a hard life.

NO LIFE IN THE DEEP?

Over 2,000 years ago, a Roman philosopher called Pliny wondered if the deep ocean had any life at all. In fact, for most of history many people believed it was a dead zone. But in 1872 scientists set sail for the deepest part of the ocean, and discovered more than 4,000 previously unknown species living in the ocean deep! The scientists on this expedition sailed 70,000 nautical miles over a period lasting more than four years, and even accidentally discovered the Challenger Deep—the deepest part of the deepest trench in the ocean!

SCIENTISTS HARDLY EVER SEE DEEP-SEA CREATURES

Very few of us have ever visited the deep, so there are hardly any eyewitness accounts of its wonders. Almost everything we know about deep-sea creatures comes from cameras mounted on submarine robots, or from dredges (scoops that pick up the sea floor) and nets that bring up dead or dying creatures for scientists to study.

EXPLORER SPOTLIGHT

WILL **YOU** BE THE WORLD'S NEXT DEEP-SEA EXPLORER?

THE FIRST EVER DIVE

The first person ever to visit the deep ocean was William Beebe. In the late 1920s he had a steel sphere built, which he called the Bathysphere. It was just 4.75 feet across, and two people had to squeeze into the tiny space through a narrow hatch that was bolted behind them. Then it was lowered into the sea on a cable. It must have been so scary to make that first ever trip in 1930! But being scared didn't put William Beebe off. Between 1930 and 1934, Beebe and his team repeatedly entered the Bathysphere and delved into the deep ocean off Nonsuch Island, near Bermuda. The deepest they went was 3,028 feet.

GLORIA HOLLISTER
THE FIRST FEMALE DEEP-SEA EXPLORER

On June 11, 1930, Gloria Hollister, one of Beebe's assistants, descended in the Bathysphere to 410 feet. It was her 30th birthday and she set a depth record for women! She also developed a method of treating deep-sea fish that made their skin and muscles invisible, revealing their skeletons for scientists to study.

VICTOR VESCOVO

DEEP-SEA ADVENTURER

Deep-sea explorer Victor Vescovo holds the record for the deepest dive ever made by a human. Victor managed to reach 35,872 feet down in the Mariana Trench (the deepest trench in the ocean)! Unfortunately, he found more than he bargained for. Resting at the bottom of the most remote place on Earth, he came across what looked like a piece of plastic. Now we know where some of the millions of tons of our plastic trash ends up. Victor did not let this sad discovery spoil the specialness of being so far down in the deep blue; instead, he had the happiest and most peaceful moment. He sat back, looked out of the viewing portal and enjoyed a sandwich as he drifted just above the deepest place on Earth.

JAMES CAMERON

AND THE DEEP SEA CHALLENGER

It's not just scientists who explore the deep sea. Anyone with the passion, a sense of adventure and enough money can venture down—even film directors! James Cameron is a Canadian film director and on March 26, 2012, he piloted a 24 foot-long submersible to the deepest place on Earth, the Challenger Deep. The submersible was named the Deep Sea Challenger, and was made with very special material that was able to withstand the intense pressures of the deep. This vessel was built in Sydney, Australia. It carried scientific sampling equipment and cameras and took 2 hours and 36 minutes to go from the surface to the bottom.

THE MYSTERY OF THE OCEAN DEEP

Less than 1 percent of the deep ocean has been mapped, and most creatures down here remain unknown. Scientists have examined 900 hours of video footage taken in the deep ocean, around the Pacific Islands. They captured images of 347,000 deep-sea creatures, from tiny worms to sharks the size of a truck. But less than one-fifth of the creatures photographed could be identified!

HAVE MORE PEOPLE BEEN TO THE MOON OR THE BOTTOM OF THE SEA?

Believe it or not, more people have been to the moon than to the deepest part of the ocean! The twelve people to have walked on the moon are Neil Armstrong, "Buzz" Aldrin, "Pete" Conrad, Alan Bean, Alan Shepard Jr, Edgar Mitchell, David Scott, James Irwin, John Young, Charles Duke, Eugene Cernan and Harrison Schmitt. The eight people who have descended to the deepest part of the ocean—and lived to tell the tale—are Jacques Piccard, Don Walsh, James Cameron, Victor Vescovo, Patrick Lahey, Jonathan Struwe, John Ramsay and Dr Alan Jamieson. Will you be the world's ninth deep-sea explorer?

TWILIGHT ZONE

The world's oceans might look large and formless, like a big boring puddle, but they're not! Just like on the land, oceans are full of many different kinds of environments. There are underwater mountain ranges, warm and shallow coasts, huge trenches and deep dark seas. The ocean changes not just from one side of the planet to the other, but also from the top to the bottom. Ocean-dwelling creatures are often tailored to live in one specific environment, whether that be in one part of the world or in one of the ocean's zones.

Have you ever traveled on a cruise ship? Or been out to sea on a ferry or boat? I've been on many cruises and boats while sailing across the world's oceans. If the water was clear and sunlit all the way down, you'd be able to see an incredible landscape of submarine ridges, canyons and mountains below. If you do go on a cruise, use your imagination to think about what lies miles below you, and what your ship would look like from the bottom of the sea!

The Twilight Zone is the first zone of the deep sea, extending from 650 to 3,300 feet in depth. It can get cold in parts, with the water temperature varying from 40 degrees Fahrenheit to 68 degrees Fahrenheit. There is light down here, but it is a tiny fraction of that at the surface—less than 1 percent. Animals that live in the Twilight Zone often have very large eyes to make up for it. Down here you will find creatures with eyes the size of dinner plates, as well as animals even longer than a blue whale. You will also discover some of the most unusual sharks known to science—those with huge cavernous mouths, goblin-like noses or snake-like bodies.

Life is abundant in the Twilight Zone. Some scientists estimate there are more fish living in the Twilight Zone than in the rest of the ocean put together. One Twilight Zone fish, the bristlemouth, is just an inch long. There are more bristlemouths than any other species of fish, bird or mammal. Quadrillions of them live in the Twilight Zone! The great deal of life in the Twilight Zone supports the zones below it, which are not as abundant. Dead animals and poo from creatures near the surface, known as marine snow, float all the way down to the depths, feeding the ocean's inhabitants deep down below. Just who are these inhabitants?

READ ON TO FIND OUT!

HAIRY SEADEVIL

CAULOPHRYNE POLYNEMA

The **hairy seadevil** is a sad-looking creature. It swims along slowly, appearing half-dead, with its large fins almost rotting off. It's covered in long hairs that stick out rather messily, and a big pot belly hangs down from its black body. This weird-looking animal is found all over the world's oceans, at up to 4,100 feet down.

← LURE

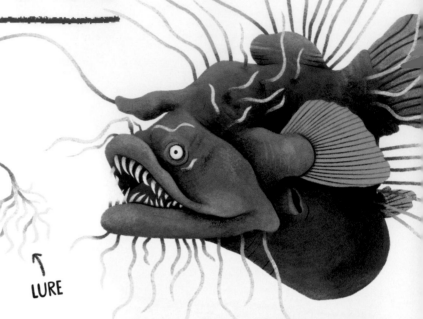

SNACK TIME!

The **hairy seadevil** is a type of anglerfish. Unlike most anglerfish, it does not have a glowing lure to attract prey. **On the end of its lure there are just more hairs!** Its masses of messy hair can detect small changes in the surrounding water pressure when anything travels near, including prey. So the hairy seadevil just lies in wait in the dark, cold depths, hoping an innocent animal will swim by and become a tasty snack!

SNEAKY!

CLINGING ON FOR DEAR LIFE

Female **hairy seadevils**, at 5.5 inches long, are giant in comparison to the half-inch-long males. The two sexes look like different species, and they also have two contrasting ways of life. The females live like most other fish, swimming freely and finding their own food. But the dwarfed males do not want a life of freedom. When they find a female they bite her, never to let go! The male's face melts into the female's skin, and the two seadevils become one. The males live out their lives attached to the female, being fed by her body. This is known as a parasitic male.

PINCUSHION SEADEVIL

NEOCERATIAS SPINIFER

The **pincushion seadevil** is also known as the needlebeard. It has a long body and a face with thin teeth that stick out in funny directions. It would be hard to eat with teeth like that, and scientists aren't sure how it does it! Females are around 4 inches long; the males are much smaller and attached to the female. This is another example of a parasitic male.

BIG RED JELLYFISH

TIBURONIA GRANROJO

This **big red jellyfish** is about 3 feet across and was first discovered off the coast of California. It has since been spotted in the waters off Hawaii. It lives 160 to 4,900 feet deep and was first seen by scientists using an underwater camera. When it approached the camera it reminded them of a big red spaceship coming in to land!

MANY QUESTIONS TO ANSWER

Scientists still know little about this big red jelly. How and what does it eat? Does it have any predators? How does it reproduce? Maybe you will be the one to find out!

NO TENTACLES FOR ME

The **big red jellyfish** is unlike almost all other jellyfish in that it has no tentacles. It is one of only a few species of tentacle-less jellies, including a deadly species of **Irukandji jellyfish** and a jelly called **Cassiopea** that sits upside down on the sea floor! Instead of tentacles, the big red jellyfish has several thick arms that it uses to catch its prey. While tentacles hang down from the edge of a jellyfish's body, known as the bell, oral arms hang down from inside the bell. The oral arms are used to bring food to the jellyfish's mouth. Oddly, the big red jelly can have anywhere from four to seven arms!

wow!

17

WHIP DRAGONFISH

GRAMMATOSTOMIAS FLAGELLIBARBA

Many species of dragonfish lurk in the waters of the Twilight Zone. They are a small yet fearsome predator. The **whip dragonfish** is less than 8 inches long, but it sure looks gruesome. It has a long, dark body and very large teeth. It can be found at depths of 5,000 feet and lives in the north and western Atlantic Ocean, as well as the Gulf of Mexico.

THE LIGHT BULB DANCE

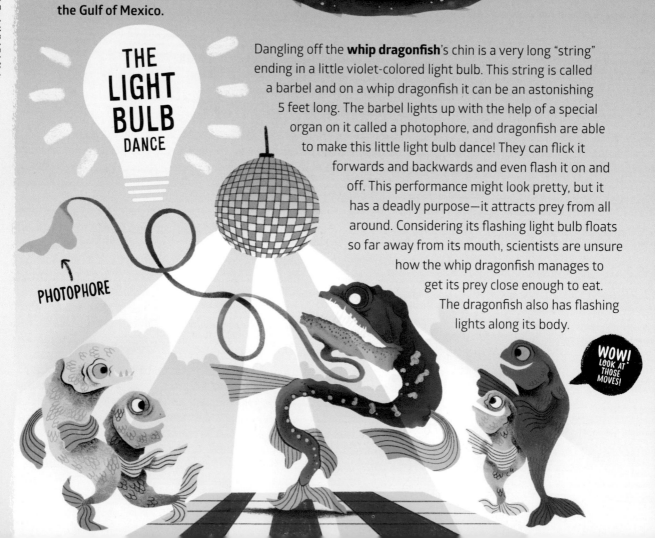

← PHOTOPHORE

Dangling off the **whip dragonfish**'s chin is a very long "string" ending in a little violet-colored light bulb. This string is called a barbel and on a whip dragonfish it can be an astonishing 5 feet long. The barbel lights up with the help of a special organ on it called a photophore, and dragonfish are able to make this little light bulb dance! They can flick it forwards and backwards and even flash it on and off. This performance might look pretty, but it has a deadly purpose—it attracts prey from all around. Considering its flashing light bulb floats so far away from its mouth, scientists are unsure how the whip dragonfish manages to get its prey close enough to eat. The dragonfish also has flashing lights along its body.

WOW! LOOK AT THOSE MOVES!

HIDDEN DINNER

The prey of the **whip dragonfish** often make their own light, which can keep shining even after they've been eaten! So the whip dragonfish has a very black stomach to make sure it does not draw attention to itself after swallowing a bright meal. It must stay hidden from its own predators, or it will become someone else's dinner!

TRANSPARENT TEETH

Scientists have studied the teeth of one species of **dragonfish** using a powerful microscope. They found that the teeth are made up of very tiny crystals. These crystals are arranged in such a way that it makes the teeth transparent (see-through) and very strong. Its teeth were found to be stronger than those of a **piranha** or even a **great white shark**! Scientists think the teeth are transparent so they can disappear into the darkness of the ocean, helping to hide this fearsome hunter in the deep.

RABBIT-FISH

CHIMAERA MONSTROSA

The **rabbit-fish** is no pet! It is a kind of chimaera (a group of animals related to sharks and rays). It has two large eyes and a rabbit-like snout. With a whip-like tail, these creatures can reach up to 5 feet long.

These fish are often found in the eastern Atlantic Ocean. They live at depths of 130 to 5,250 feet, and use their two large side fins to glide along the sea floor. Rabbit-fish like to stay near the bottom so they can search for invertebrate prey to feed on. Unlike most other fish, rabbit-fish don't have teeth. Instead, they have three rows of teeth plates that they use to crush and grind the hard parts of their prey.

OUCH!

Poking out of the fin on the **rabbit-fish**'s back (their dorsal fin) is a very large spine. This spine is a little venomous and is capable of injuring any predator that comes too close.

IMAGINE IF YOUR BUNNY HAD A TAIL LIKE THIS INSTEAD OF ITS CUTE PUFFBALL!

19

SLENDER SNIPE EEL

NEMICHTHYS SCOLOPACEUS

This creature is also known as a threadfish, because it is almost as slender as a piece of string! It has a thin, long snout that looks like the narrow beak of a bird. The ends of its jaws curve backwards, and don't meet even when its mouth is closed. The **slender snipe eel** is found in oceans around the world, preferring waters that are 1,300 to 3,300 feet deep. It has also been found in depths of up to 13,000 feet.

THE SLEEK SLENDER SNIPE EEL (TRY SAYING THAT THREE TIMES QUICKLY!) REACHES OVER 4 FEET IN LENGTH AND WEIGHS VERY LITTLE.

THE LONGEST SPINE

The **slender snipe eel** has the most vertebrae of any animal on Earth—over 740! Vertebrae are the small bones that make up the backbone. Humans only have 33.

ANTENNAE-SNATCHING TEETH!

Animal teeth are different shapes because animals specialize in eating different things. The **slender snipe eel**'s jaws are full of many tiny teeth that point backwards. These teeth are covered in hooks, which help it keep hold of its prey. The slender snipe eel's favorite food is tiny deep-sea shrimps. When a little shrimp swims past, its antennae get caught in the slender snipe eel's teeth. So the clever slender snipe eels swim slowly along with their mouths open, hoping to catch a delicious meal!

WHERE ARE MY DENTURES?

When male **slender snipe eels** grow old, they lose all their teeth and their jaws shorten. This does not happen to the females, so scientists once thought they were two different species. It is thought the older males lose their teeth and have shortened jaws because they use up all their energy mating. In fact, they're more interested in mating than eating!

OK, I'M DONE!

When breeding, each **slender snipe eel** releases its eggs, if it's female, or its sperm, if it's male, into the water. This is called broadcast spawning. The eggs and sperm have to find one another in the big ocean, and not all of them do. (This method is not as reliable as internal fertilization, which is how humans reproduce!) Once the slender snipe eel eggs are fertilized by the sperm, they float on the top of the sea until the babies are ready to hatch. Freshly hatched baby slender snipe eels look just like tiny leaves! All of this reproduction is a huge effort for the slender snipe eel. It is thought they have just one attempt at mating, and then they become so exhausted they die.

BUTT THROAT

The butt of the **slender snipe eel** is not where you would expect. It's right up near its throat! Its intestines actually stretch down its body, then bend right back up again towards its butt. I am glad I am not a slender snipe eel . . . imagine having to poo so close to where your mouth is!

YUCK!

EEL TUBE-EYE

STYLEPHORUS CHORDATUS

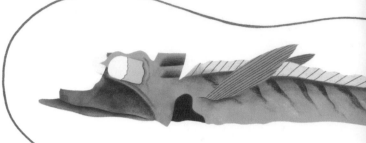

The **eel tube-eye** looks a bit like a strand of spaghetti wearing binoculars! Its noodle-like body is 1 foot long, ending in extremely long tailfins that triple its size and make it about 3 feet long, all up. It lives in tropical and subtropical waters up to 2,600 feet down, in the Atlantic Ocean and eastern Pacific Ocean. The eel tube-eye migrates towards the surface of the Twilight Zone at night to feed on tiny crustaceans called copepods.

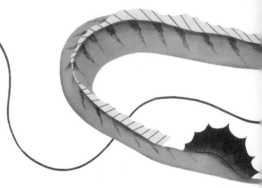

DON'T SUCK ME IN!

EXPLORER SP🔍TLIGHT

THE GREATEST MIGRATION ON EARTH

A huge variety of creatures, including the **eel tube-eye**, come up every day from the Twilight Zone towards the ocean's surface. The migration was first discovered during World War II, when the US Navy looked for enemy submarines using sonar. They saw what they thought was the sea floor, around 1,600 feet down, slowly rise to the surface at night. It wasn't the sea floor at all, but billions of creatures of the Twilight Zone! The creatures—from plankton to fish, jellyfish and squids—migrate to the surface at night, when it's safe for them to find food. Meanwhile, whales, tuna, sharks and swordfish, usually on the surface, dive down into the Twilight Zone's depths to find food.

As it waits for its prey, the **eel tube-eye** rests its head higher up in the water than its body, like a dangling deadly snake. As its head is facing upwards, its eyes can look high above, seeking out something to eat. Once it has found what it is looking for, its mouth expands by up to 38 times its size! It can do this very quickly and, as its mouth grows, water rapidly flows in. This water slurps in all those poor little crustaceans close enough to get caught in the current!

WHAT ARE YOU?

The **eel tube-eye** was discovered back in 1798 by George Shaw. George was an English biologist and he thought the fish was so odd that he almost mistakenly identified it as a type of amphibian! Amphibians are animals like frogs and salamanders. George's eel tube-eye was the only one available for scientists to study for over 100 years, until someone caught another in 1908.

BINOCULAR EYES

The **eel tube-eye** has cylindrical eyes that are highly sensitive. They can see all sorts of colors in near darkness, but are especially sensitive to blue or green light. Many fish produce their own blue or green light to find prey or attract a mate, so it is likely the tube-eye uses its sensitive eyes to spot prey or predators.

BLOBFISH

PSYCHROLUTES MARCIDUS

Once called the world's ugliest animal, this fish is surely not going to win any beauty pageants. With a very broad and bulbous head, it reaches up to 15 inches across. There are 30 species of **blobfish**; the first was discovered over 150 years ago. *Psychrolutes marcidus* has only been found in the waters off southern Australia from 2,000 to 4,000 feet deep. Blobfish float close to the sea floor and are opportunistic feeders. This means they take a bite of whatever little creature they may come across.

LIFE UNDER PRESSURE

Up on the surface, the **blobfish** looks like formless jelly. But in its natural habitat its body is not as blobby as you would think. The pressure is much greater down there and its body is supported by the surrounding water. Down on the sea floor, the blobfish looks much more like other fish.

MR. BLOBBY

These poor fish got their nickname in 2003 when scientists off the coast of New Zealand hauled one aboard. When it reached the surface they were shocked at its blobby appearance!

23

MEGAMOUTH

MEGACHASMA PELAGIOS

EVEN REALLY BIG ANIMALS CAN GO UNDISCOVERED IN THE DEEP SEA!

Despite its huge size, this funny-looking shark was only discovered in 1979! It is very rarely seen and scientists have documented all 69 sightings of the animal. The **megamouth** is one of the largest sharks in the world, reaching up to 2,600 pounds and 18 feet in length. It has a big, bulbous head and a stubby nose. It has been found all over the world at depths of 300 to 3,300 feet.

SMALL PREY FOR A BIG MOUTH

These beasts swim along with their huge mouths wide open. But these odd-looking sharks are nothing to be afraid of—they definitely won't be swallowing you whole! They have long, soft bodies with wide front fins, and their teeth are tiny. They are filter feeders, filtering large amounts of sea water to find enough little critters to keep them full. There are only three species of shark in the world that feed like this: **whale sharks**, **basking sharks** and the **megamouth**. During the night, the megamouth chases after crowds of krill (little shrimps) and jellyfish up at the surface of the ocean, then dives deeper during the day. The inside of its mouth is dotted with glowing spots, which entice its prey to come closer.

BABY FOOD

The megamouth gives birth to live young. As soon as they pop out, they are able to filter-feed themselves.

COOL!

WHERE CAN I SEE ONE?

In 1988 a **megamouth** was found washed up on the shore of Mandurah Beach, off the coast of Western Australia. You can see it in all its glory, preserved in a giant tank at the Western Australian Maritime Museum in Fremantle. Preserved megamouths are also found in other places, including the Bishop Museum in Hawaii, the Natural History Museum of Los Angeles County, and the Toba Aquarium in Japan. However, not all megamouths in museums are on display; some are kept safe in collections out of public view.

EXPLORER SPOTLIGHT

FIRST DISCOVERY

The **megamouth** was first discovered by accident. It was 1976 and the US Navy was looking for enemy submarines off the coast of Hawaii. During a military operation, several parachutes were sunk, acting as anchors for special equipment. When these parachutes were pulled up, the crew saw that a giant megamouth was attached to one—it had swallowed a parachute whole! No one had ever seen anything quite like it, and it was sent to a museum in Hawaii to be preserved. Unfortunately, no one was to know of this important discovery for some time. The shark was found during a classified operation, meaning everything had to be kept secret! It was seven years before scientists were able to report this exciting finding to the world and give the new species a name. Since then, several megamouths have been caught by deep-sea fishing boats.

GOBLIN SHARK

MITSUKURINA OWSTONI

This bizarre shark is found across the world's oceans from 300 to 4,300 feet deep.

On the surface of this nose are many tiny holes that have a fancy name: the ampullae of Lorenzini. The holes are filled with mucus and contain special electric receptors that are used by the shark to find fish and squids to eat. **YUCK!**

I'M BACK!

The **goblin shark** was thought to have become extinct 100 million years ago—but then a living specimen was discovered in 1898!

SLINGSHOT
FEEDING

In 2008 in Tokyo Bay, off the coast of Japan, scientists were lucky enough to film this shark's unusual feeding behavior. The **goblin shark** should really be called the gobbling shark. It can speedily push those scary jaws far in front of its face, gobbling up its unfortunate prey. Its jaws are attached to its skull by flexible cartilage and ligaments, so they can fling forward as if they are spring-loaded! The goblin shark pushes its jaws forward farther and faster than any other shark in the world. This technique helps it to catch fast-moving prey. It has many teeth that curve towards the back of its mouth, useful for preventing its prey from escaping. It is not a fast swimmer and probably takes its prey by surprise.

I'M OFF!

BLUNTNOSE SIXGILL SHARK

HEXANCHUS GRISEUS

The **bluntnose sixgill shark** has more in common with prehistoric sharks than those in the modern day. It looks a lot like its ancestors that lived up to 200 million years ago—way before Tyrannosaurus rex roamed the land! Most species of shark have five sets of gills, but this guy has six. Sharks with six sets of gills are known as a primitive species—one that has not changed in a long time. Most modern-day sharks have two fins on their backs called dorsal fins. The bluntnose sixgill has only one. It's a big, green-eyed shark, reaching almost 16 feet in length and weighing 1,100 pounds. It lives in tropical and temperate oceans around the world from 65 to 8,200 feet deep.

650 TO 3,300 FEET DEEP

DID YOU KNOW?

A baby shark is called a pup! The **bluntnose sixgill** gives birth to 40 to 110 pups at once, and these can be up to 2.5 feet long. Imagine having that many siblings!

EXPLORER SPOTLIGHT

SHARK TAGGING

Not much is known about the **bluntnose sixgill**. In 2019, in an effort to find out more, a group of scientists descended into the depths of the ocean in a submarine. They were hoping to attract a shark with a piece of bait and waited patiently for one to appear. When in sight, the scientists attached a tag to the male's fin. A tag can stay attached to an animal for around three months and can give scientists all kinds of information. Once a tag is retrieved it can let us know how deep the shark swam and how light and cold the water was. It'll be fascinating to see what this tag reveals!

FRILLED SHARK

CHLAMYDOSELACHUS ANGUINEUS

The **frilled shark** is rarely seen by humans. It is known to live in both the Atlantic Ocean and Pacific Ocean from 160 to 3,900 feet deep. Just like its cousin, the **bluntnose sixgill shark**, it has six sets of gills and is a primitive shark. Its appearance has barely changed in millions of years. Scientists don't really know why an animal would remain relatively unchanged for so long. It could be because it lives in a very stable environment, like the deep sea, or due to a lack of competition from other animals in finding food. Why change when there's no need to?

A SORRY TAIL

Several **frilled sharks** have been seen missing their tails, which were likely bitten off by another kind of shark.

OUCH!

← UP TO 6.5 FEET IN LENGTH!

THIS ELONGATED CREATURE WITH FRILL-LINED GILLS LOOKS MORE LIKE A DECORATED EEL THAN A SHARK.

A VERY LONG PREGNANCY

The amount of time an animal grows its baby inside is called the gestation period. For humans, it usually takes nine months until the baby can pop out; for **elephants** it is 22 months. But down in the deep sea, life moves slowly. Scientists estimate that the **frilled shark** has a gestation period of 42 months.

A NEW SWIMMING STROKE

The **frilled shark** is one of the slowest species of shark—and it seems to have taken swimming lessons from a snake! When it's not hovering in the water it swims in a very unusual fashion, curving its body from side to side just like a sea snake.

SO MANY TEETH!

The mouth of this slippery shark is at the end of its snout, not down below like most sharks' mouths. It has 300 teeth set out in 25 rows, all facing backwards. These backward-facing teeth mean there's no escaping if you happen to get caught.

SECRET SWALLOWERS

GULP!

FRILLED SHARKS ARE THE SECRET SWALLOWERS OF THE DEEP!

No one has ever seen one feeding, so we are not quite sure how they do it. One way scientists can find out what **frilled sharks** eat is by looking at their stomachs. Squids, other sharks and fish have all been found in their stomachs, and all have been intact. This means these secretive frilled sharks swallow their prey whole.

GIANT SQUID

ARCHITEUTHIS DUX

Many a story has been told of **giant squids** sinking ships in far-off seas, with sailors needing to be rescued in treacherous waters. Although no longer believed to be a man-eating sea monster, this is still an impressive beast. The giant squid reaches up to 42 feet in length and has been caught at depths of between 1,300 and 2,600 feet in oceans around the world.

DEEP-SEA TORPEDO

The **giant squid**'s body is shaped like a jumbo torpedo. But it doesn't have many muscles, and its body—which is called the mantle—has two small fins attached. All of this means that it probably can't swim very fast.

FEEDING TENTACLES

CHIEF SQUID

The giant squid's scientific name, *Architeuthis dux*, means chief squid.

DID YOU KNOW?

It is thought giant squids reproduce just once in their entire lives.

EACH GIANT SQUID EYE IS 12 INCHES ACROSS—THAT'S AS BIG AS A HUMAN HEAD!

TREMENDOUS TENTACLES

Emerging from the squid's mantle are eight long arms and two even longer feeding tentacles. Two-thirds of the squid's length is made up of its extra-long feeding tentacles. These tentacles are different to its eight arms in that they end in a 3-foot-long club that is full of hundreds of deadly suckers, which are useful for capturing and holding on to the squid's prey. Squids can use these feeding tentacles to catch prey that is over 30 feet away. Once it's caught, the eight arms move the unlucky prey towards its mouth.

HOW LONG DO GIANT SQUIDS LIVE?

Scientists can find out how old a squid is by counting the growth rings in a special body part called a statolith. Each squid has two hard, grain-sized statoliths located at the bottom of its brain. Squids use statoliths to balance in the ocean—it's how they know which way is up and which is down. Surprisingly, **giant squids** were found to live to only five years of age. This means a squid must grow unbelievably quickly to reach its colossal size in under five years. Imagine all the food it has to eat!

SQUIDS THROUGH THE AGES

Throughout history there have been reports of people coming across **giant squids**. One of the earliest is from a Roman philosopher called Pliny the Elder, who lived over 2,000 years ago. He described seeing a 700-pound beast with large, club-like tentacles.

SMILE FOR THE CAMERA!

It was not until 2004 that the first photographs of a live **giant squid** were taken. Japanese researchers sent a camera and baited hook 3,000 feet down, and waited patiently for one to appear.

In 2006, scientists managed to get video footage of a live squid, but it took six more years for a giant squid to be filmed deep down in its natural habitat. In 2012, and then again in 2019, scientists used a bait with a glowing lure to attract a giant squid close enough to their sunken video camera. You can find these videos online and see this sea monster for yourself!

WHAT DOES A GIANT SQUID EAT?

No one has seen a **giant squid** hunt for prey in its natural habitat. We know what they like to eat from studying squids that have washed ashore. Rays, large fish, and even other giant squids have been found inside the stomachs of giant squids. A giant squid was once found washed up on shore with only giant sucker marks where its feeding tentacles used to be. This poor squid's feeding tentacles would have been lost, along with its meal, when another, bigger squid ripped them both away.

DEADLY BEAK

The **giant squid** has a hard, sharp beak hidden away between its tentacles. It uses this beak to tear its prey into smaller pieces. As if this wasn't scary enough, inside its beak it has a tongue-like organ called a radula. The radula is covered in many tiny teeth that help the squid break apart its prey even more.

YIKES!

VAMPIRE SQUID

VAMPYROTEUTHIS INFERNALIS

The **vampire squid** reaches a length of 12 inches and is about the size of a football. Despite its name, it is neither a squid nor a vampire! It's not an octopus either. It is so unusual that scientists have placed it into its own group. Its body is black to red in color with two ear-like fins that stick out. It has eight arms that have a very unusual feature: they are connected by webbing, just like a duck's foot! Along with its arms, it also has two tentacles. The vampire squid is usually found 2,000 to 3,900 feet down, in temperate and tropical waters throughout the world's oceans.

1

WORLD-RECORD HOLDER

Although its eyes are not nearly as big as the giant or colossal squid's eyes (see pages 30 and 65), the **vampire squid** holds its own world record. It has the biggest eyes (1 inch) relative to body size of any animal in the world.

MYSTERIOUS . . .

The **vampire squid** was first discovered over 100 years ago, but it took until 2012 for scientists to figure out what and how it eats!

MARINE SNOW

Marine snow is made up of particles that float down from way up above. These particles can be little pieces of dead animals or even bits of poo! The **vampire squid** uses thin "strings" that extend out from its body to catch this snow. These strings can stretch out to eight times the length of the squid's body, acting like a fishing line. Before it can eat the marine snow, the squid uses its arms to scrape it into a big ball of mucus. Then the mucus ball goes into its mouth!

YUCK!

PINEAPPLE POSTURE

When the **vampire squid** feels threatened, it makes what is known as a "pineapple posture." It stretches its webbed arms over its head to protect itself. Its tentacles are lined with rows of little spines called cirri and they stick out so it looks just like a pineapple! Light-producing organs cover almost all of the vampire squid's body, with the brightest ones at the tips of its arms. The vampire squid is able to flash these lights like an explosion of fireworks, confusing any predator that comes too close. If it feels in real danger it has one last defense in its arsenal. The vampire squid is able to squirt out sticky clouds of bright mucus, shocking its attacker and allowing it to swim to safety in the confusion.

AN UNFAIR REPUTATION

The **vampire squid**'s scientific name, *Vampyroteuthis infernalis*, means vampire squid from hell. So I don't blame you if you're expecting this creature to be a menacing predator of the deep. This little guy is far from it, though! Despite its name, the vampire squid does not feed on blood. Unlike squids and octopuses, it prefers a much more harmless way of eating, and that is by collecting marine snow.

650 TO 3,300 FEET DEEP

SWIMMING LIKE DUMBO

Adult **vampire squid** use their big, ear-like fins to slowly flap themselves along in the water.

JEWEL SQUID

HISTIOTEUTHIS REVERSA

Like a beautiful glistening gem, the **jewel squid** is striking in its looks. It is a common species of squid and is found in the Atlantic Ocean at depths of 1,600 to 6,600 feet.

A COCKEYED SQUID

Is that a squid squinting at me? No, it's just a cockeyed squid! The **jewel squid** belongs to a group called the cockeyed squids, which are named for their two differently sized eyes. They have one large eye that is always pointed towards the ocean surface, searching for predators. On the other side is a smaller eye that scans down below for any flashes of light from another animal.

A LIGHT SNACK

The **jewel squid** is a favorite prey for many larger animals, and has been found in the stomachs of sperm whales, dolphins and sharks.

DIAMONDS ARE A GIRL'S BEST FRIEND

What look like jewels are actually the squid's light organs, known as photophores. Both female and male **jewel squids** have these light organs covering their bodies, but they look a little different from one another. When the female is fully grown her body is more elongated, and she adorns herself with extra "jewels" along her tentacles and body. The light organs of the jewel squid are special, in that they are more complicated than those found on some other squids. They can be large or small, and have reflectors as well as special muscles so they can aim the light in a specific direction. They even have colored coverings so that the squid can change the light's color! Instead of being used to attract prey, like the light-lures of some **anglerfish** (see page 43), they are likely used to attract a mate or even confuse predators.

TELESCOPE OCTOPUS

AMPHITRETUS PELAGICUS

A good set of large eyes is very useful in the Twilight Zone. Large eyes maximize the light an animal is able to see, helping it find prey and avoid predators. But instead of having large eyes, the **telescope octopus** has a different technique to help it see—its eyes sit on stalks! These stalks can even move around, so the octopus can see in many different directions. The telescope octopus is the only known octopus to have eyes like this. Unlike many other octopuses that prefer staying closer to the sea floor, the telescope octopus can be found hundreds of feet above the bottom.

650 TO 3,300 FEET DEEP

FLANNERY FILE

FOSSIL TRAVELLERS FROM THE DEEP

There are not a lot of fossils of deep-sea creatures. They don't have many bones, and the sea floor from the deep ocean is rarely preserved as fossil rocks. But sometimes a visitor from the deep is preserved in shallower waters. I found one such creature on a fossil-finding trip with my children—it was hidden in some rocks on a cliff in Victoria, Australia. It was a **nautilus** (a shelled animal related to squids and octopuses), 50 million years old and as big as a soccer ball. Scientists studied its shell and found out that it grew in much colder water than the fossils of other creatures that were preserved around it. So it must have come from far away—from the cold waters that abound in the deep.

STAYING HIDDEN

The **telescope octopus** is about 8 inches long and is found 500 to 8,200 feet deep in the Indian Ocean and the Pacific Ocean. It has a gelatinous, see-through body, just like a jellyfish, and you can see all of its organs inside! Between its eight legs is a thin webbing. Apart from its eyes and stomach it looks almost invisible as it swims along in the ocean. When it swims it can stretch out long, which might help it stay hidden from predators that are searching for their next meal.

GLASS SPONGE

HEXACTINELLIDA

Sponges can look a little confusing. Are they an animal, a plant, or something to do the dishes with?! People often don't realize that sponges are animals. Sponges were some of the first multicellular life (life with more than one cell, like all animals and plants) to evolve on Earth over 600 million years ago. Sponges roamed the ancient seas long before any animals that you might be familiar with even existed. Animals did not begin to live on land until a little over 400 million years ago, and dinosaurs came along around 240 million years ago.

There are over 500 species of **glass sponge** and they are found in oceans all over the world. Most live between 1,300 and 3,000 feet deep, but some have been found as deep as 19,700 feet.

GLASS SPONGES CAN VARY GREATLY IN SIZE; THE SMALLEST ARE LESS THAN HALF AN INCH AND THE LARGEST CAN GROW TO ALMOST 6.5 FEET LONG.

A STRONG, SAFE BODY

Some species of **glass sponge** rise up from the sea floor, like a white flowering plant standing out from their dark surroundings. The glass sponge is unlike any other sponge; it is not soft and squidgy, but glassy and hard. It looks a lot like a fragile vase, but it is far from it. The sponge's skeleton is made of tiny needles of silica. Silica is a hard mineral that is commonly found as sand grains on the beach, and is used to make the windows in your home. A body made of silica is one of great strength and flexibility. This skeleton protects the glass sponge from many predators.

MY GLASS-WALLED HOME

Glass sponges provide shelter for many other animals, with fish and crustaceans often seen swimming close by. One species of glass sponge, the **Venus' flower basket**, is very important to a type of shrimp that calls the inside of the sponge home. These shrimps keep their sponge home clean and tidy, and in return they receive safety and food from the sponge.

When the shrimps are very small, they enter through holes in the glass body of the sponge, living out their entire lives within the sponge's walls. They get so big they are unable to escape, and their home becomes a cage. When the shrimps have babies, they release them into the surrounding ocean so that they can find their own sponge home!

CUTE!

HOW DO SPONGES HELP HUMANS?

Because of the great strength and flexibility of their skeletons, **glass sponges** are studied by scientists interested in making better materials for humankind. These materials can be used for things like the internet, to help improve our communications over longer distances and at faster speeds! Even though the internet might appear invisible to you, it is actually a vast network of computers. These computers need to be joined by cables, and what these cables are made of can greatly improve the speed of information. Guess where many of these cables are located? That's right, under the sea! There are well over 600,000 miles of cables resting on the sea floor, connecting all of the world's continents.

FILTER FEEDERS

Glass sponges are filter feeders, meaning they pass large amounts of sea water through their bodies to find tiny bacteria and plankton to eat. There is still a lot we do not know about the many species of glass sponge, like how they make their own babies, what exactly they like to eat and where they like to live.

SIPHONOPHORES

I bet you have never heard of **siphonophores**, but there are many weird and cool things to learn about these critters! They are related to jellyfish and sea anemones and are very odd animals. There are 175 species and they come in all sorts of shapes, sizes and colors. Some have a stem attached to a floating bubble. Some are elongated and thin, with lots of trailing tentacles, and some are more round in shape. They can be white, red, orange or even purple. Many species use their tentacles to attach to the sea floor, several types prefer to swim along the surface, and some feel most at home in the waters in between.

Siphonophores are found in all of the world's oceans and use jet propulsion to move, pushing out water at high speed behind them.

HOW DO SLURP GUNS HELP SCIENTISTS?

Siphonophores are hard to collect to study. They are very delicate, and fall apart when scientists try to catch them. Last century, deep-sea creatures were commonly caught using a big net that was trawled beneath a boat. This net was able to find a lot of animals, but it often destroyed the fragile ones on the way up. Scientists can now use equipment attached to deep-sea submersibles to carefully catch creatures down below. This equipment includes things such as slurp guns, which use suction to catch swimming animals! They can then be studied on the surface.

WHEN THE HUNTER BECOMES THE HUNTED

One species of deep-sea **siphonophores** has developed a clever, sneaky way to find prey in the vast ocean. On each of its tentacles is a bright red light that it uses as a decoy. It twitches the lights so that when they move they look like little crustaceans. And who do you think will come looking for a little crustacean to eat? Other fish! These unsuspecting fish think they are about to get their next meal. Instead, it's the siphonophore who is about to get dinner!

LIGHT-PRODUCING PREDATORS

Siphonophores are predators, and use their stinging cells to catch small crustaceans and fish. Some siphonophores can make green, blue or even red light to attract prey. Most siphonophores sit and wait for their prey to come to them. They cast their tentacles out like a big net and wait for their prey to be accidentally stung.

SUPER-ORGANISMS

Incredibly, a **siphonophore** is not one creature, but thousands of tiny, specialized individuals living together! These individuals are called zoids and they are connected to make up the body of the siphonophore. The zoids are not all the same. They are each special in their own way, all serving a different purpose. Some zoids are tailored for eating, some for swimming, some for making babies and some for circulating blood!

MIDNIGHT ZONE

As we delve deeper into the sea, our surroundings become as dark as midnight on a moonless night. Everything is less comfortable: the water is as cold as a drink bottle that has been stored in your fridge (about 40 degrees) and the pressure begins to grow. The Midnight Zone ranges from 3,300 to 9,900 feet and is the first part of the ocean that no sunlight reaches at all. Many animals are daytime visitors to the Midnight Zone. They use its darkness for safety, migrating towards the surface at night to feed.

The night lasts forever in the Midnight Zone, but that does not mean there is no light at all. You will find plenty of animals there that can make their own light! This is called bioluminescence. There are over 1,500 species of bioluminescent fish. The ability to make your own light is so handy that it has evolved at least 27 separate times in the history of fish. This is truly remarkable. When an ability evolves numerous times, it means it is very useful.

The fact that over 80 percent of fish in the deep sea can twinkle means it is just about essential for survival in this inhospitable world. There are two ways an animal can have this spooky glow: it can make the light all on its own or it can use the help of bacteria. Many animals use light to attract prey, avoid predators, or even find a mate.

On our journey to the deep, food becomes harder and harder to find.

Animals in the Midnight Zone have evolved in all sorts of ways to make sure they can find and hold on to their prey. Why spend all your time searching for a meal when you can convince one to come to you? Many of the fish here have evolved methods to trick their prey into coming closer to their mouths. And once it's nearby, you'd better keep a hold of it—that's why the creatures who live here have a great deal of scary-looking teeth in jaws you'd have no hope of escaping. No one wants to miss a meal down here, no matter what its size. You never know when you might come across one again! So many of the animals have evolved ways—like having expandable jaws and stomachs—to eat prey that is bigger than themselves. Imagine eating a meal that's bigger than you are.

THAT'S A LOT OF FOOD!

ILLUMINATED NETDEVIL

LINOPHRYNE ARBORIFERA

The **illuminated netdevil** is a type of anglerfish. It is found swimming below 3,300 feet. With a glowing lure on its head and a bright bushy beard on its chin, it lights up the ocean like a Christmas tree!

LESS THAN 3 INCHES LONG!

SUCKING UP FOR LIFE

Male and female **illuminated netdevils** look very different. Most pictures you'll find will be of the female of the species—she is almost ten times the size of the male. If you look very closely, hidden on her underside will be a very small attached male. This male has no lure. He does not need one, or even a mouth, because he is completely dependent on the female for all his food.

The male has large eyes and huge nostrils, which help him seek out a female to stick himself onto. Once he has latched on to her, he actually becomes part of the female, getting all his nutrients from her. The bloodstreams of the male and female are now shared! He is known as a parasitic male, and this type of life is common in anglerfish. There is one male attached to each female. They like to place themselves upside down near the butt of the female, ready to fertilize her eggs.

WHAT A LIFE!

42

VISITOR FROM THE DEEP

Sometimes, after storms, you can find amazing things on beaches. Once I even found an **anglerfish** that had washed up. As big as my hand, it was mottled brown and yellow and had a tiny lure. It was not a deep-sea type, but people do find deep-water fish washed up after big storms or unusual conditions. Next time you are at the beach after a storm, keep an eye out for treasure from the deep sea.

LURE ME IN

There are around 160 species of **anglerfish** in the deep ocean. They are known for their big toothy grins and expandable stomachs, and they can eat prey that's much larger than them. All anglerfish have a very special body part called a lure. Have you ever been fishing and used a lure at the end of your rod? A lure is a fake bait that is used to attract an unsuspecting fish. It can be designed to look like a tasty meal, and is often shiny or brightly colored. Anglerfish use a light lure to catch their prey. Their lure sits smack-bang in the middle of their heads, glowing brightly and ever so close to their big mouths!

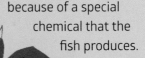

BEAM ME UP!

The **illuminated netdevil** is very rare in that it uses two ways to make its light. The light in its glowing lure is made by bacteria that live inside it. As a thanks for all their hard work, the bacteria have a nice safe place to live. The illuminated netdevil also has a bright long beard on its chin, like a fern frond dangling down. This glowing beard is used to attract prey and is bright because of a special chemical that the fish produces.

3,300 TO 9,900 FEET DEEP

FISHING CHAMPION!

WOLFTRAP SEADEVIL

LASIOGNATHUS SACCOSTOMA

The **wolftrap seadevil** is a kind of anglerfish, but with the fanciest of rods. At the end of its fishing line are three hooks that it uses to catch fish. It even casts its rod ahead of its face, just like you would if you were fly-fishing! There are eight species of wolftrap seadevil and they are found all over the world's oceans.

DID YOU KNOW?

The **wolftrap seadevil**'s scientific name means hairy-jawed sack-mouth!

LASIOGNATHUS SACCOSTOMA IS FOUND AS DEEP AS 13,000 FEET!

MIDNIGHT ZONE

NO DENTISTS IN THE DEEP

Doesn't this fish have an odd-looking head? It looks like it needs braces, it has such a big overbite! It has a long, toothy snout ending in two large nostrils. These big nostrils mean it likely has a good sense of smell. The **wolftrap seadevil** also has special sense organs down its body. It uses these to detect tiny changes in water pressure, which help it find prey.

STOPLIGHT LOOSEJAW

MALACOSTEUS NIGER

The **stoplight loosejaw** looks a bit like a traffic light. It has two light-producing organs under and behind its eyes. One light is greeny-blue and the other one is red. This fish is a species of dragonfish and is found in oceans all over the world. It can reach up to a foot long and lives up to 13,000 feet down.

NIGHT VISION

Being able to make red light is very useful down here, as most animals this deep cannot see it. For the **stoplight loosejaw**, this red light acts kind of like night-vision goggles! It can creep up on other fish and they won't be able to see a thing.

I'M HUNGRY

The jaws of the **stoplight loosejaw** are just that—loose. They are full of needle-like teeth and can stretch out very wide to catch the largest of prey. Its bottom jaw is not even covered by skin, it just opens into the water. You would be able to escape through this gap if you hadn't been impaled by their deadly teeth!

OUCH!

THEY LOVE TO EAT CRUSTACEANS AND OTHER FISH.

45

MIRRORBELLY SPOOKFISH

OPISTHOPROCTUS GRIMALDII

The **mirrorbelly spookfish** is also known as the barreleye, and there are 19 species of barreleye around the world. These have got to be the most peculiar of fish. They have huge eyes that gaze up and out of the tops of their heads! If you or I did this, all we'd see would be the dark insides of our skulls. This fish has a transparent, fluid-filled dome above its eyes. This dome helps to protect its eyes and acts as a sort of magnifying glass for light. Why do its eyes face the surface? It is likely looking for prey up above. Even weirder, once they have found what they are looking for, some species of barreleye are able to swivel their eyes to face forward. Then they can zoom off to catch their meal!

A LIGHTBULB BUTT

How's this for a party trick: the **mirrorbelly spookfish** can make light out of its butt! Right near its rear end is an organ a bit like a light bulb, where light is made by bacteria. The light can then be channelled to other parts of the fish's body. The fish can control the light through a special organ on its underside, and this is where it gets its common name, "mirrorbelly." Its scientific name, *Opisthoproctus*, means "behind anus"!

NOW YOU SEE ME . . . NOW YOU DON'T

The **mirrorbelly spookfish** has been caught in waters where some light reaches, such as in the Twilight Zone, which is above the Midnight Zone. When it visits the Twilight Zone, scientists think that its bright belly might provide protection from predators down below. As predators look up towards the bright ocean surface, the lit-up mirrorbelly would be camouflaged, meaning it can stay hidden by looking like its surroundings.

SO CLEVER!

46

WHAT'S GOING ON INSIDE YOUR HEAD?

The **jelly-faced spookfish** *(Winteria telescopa)* is another kind of barreleye. This dark-blue little guy has a see-through head that's seemingly full of jelly! Its head is so transparent that you can see all sorts of things in there, like blood vessels. It has been found at depths of 6,600 feet and is 6 inches in length. Its scientific name, *telescopa*, relates to its large, telescope-like eyes.

ELSMAN'S WHIPNOSE

GIGANTACTIS ELSMANI

Elsman's whipnose is yet another type of anglerfish, and the Midnight Zone is full of them! Fishing with a lure must be a good technique to find food. This anglerfish has a lure that looks like a long whip, ending in several little threads. Females grow to about a foot in length and have five rows of small, sharp teeth. Just like many other anglerfish, the males are much smaller—around three-quarters of an inch. They have a good sense of smell for finding females to mate with. The male Elsman's whipnoses are lucky, though. They are thought to be living free, unlike male **illuminated netdevils** (see page 42), a type of anglerfish who are stuck onto their female partners for life.

TOPSY-TURVY

It is important to be able to watch animals alive in their natural habitat, as they can behave in ways you might not expect. In 2002 scientists witnessed how one species of **Gigantactis** finds food. They watched it deep in the sea and saw that it lies in wait for its prey . . . but upside down! While upside down it sticks its fins out, leaves its mouth slightly open and places its lure out in front, hoping something might take the bait.

3,300 TO 9,900 FEET DEEP

47

COOKIECUTTER SHARK

ISISTIUS BRASILIENSIS

The **cookiecutter shark** does not like to eat cookies! It prefers to bite out morsels of flesh from much larger animals than itself. This shark grows up to 22 inches in length and during the day it lives at a depth of around 3,300 feet, migrating to the surface at night to find some dinner.

DO I SMELL COOKIES?

BRIGHT IDEA

Cookiecutter sharks have glowing bellies, which they use to attract prey. Larger fish and marine mammals might think a cookiecutter shark could be *their* next meal. But when they get too close, the cookiecutter shark jumps on!

EXPLORER SPOTLIGHT

AHHHH!

Believe it or not, there is one documented instance of a **cookiecutter shark** taking a chunk out of a human. It was 2009 and Michael Spalding, a long-distance swimmer, was swimming between two islands in Hawaii. He was enjoying the calm conditions when he felt something soft bump into him. He thought it might have been a squid until, moments later, a cookiecutter shark latched on! He was left with a wound 4 inches across and 1.5 inches deep. It took more than six months to heal. Years later, Michael finally completed his swim, this time without any shark bites.

PHEW!

HUH?

These fearsome creatures have even been known to take a bite out of a submarine!

A GHASTLY PARASITE

Cookiecutter sharks have up to 68 sharp, pointy teeth, all connected to help the shark take swift and sturdy bites. These sharks bite their prey using an unusual method. They suck onto its skin using their lips and take a deep bite with their sharp teeth. Then they twist their bodies around in a spin until a cookie-shaped chunk of flesh comes off! Cookiecutter sharks are considered a type of parasite, as their prey live on to see another day. A parasite is a creature that gets its food from another creature (known as the host), sometimes by living on or in it.

GULPER EEL

The **gulper eel** is really just a huge swimming mouth, with a long, thin tail. Its jaws are a quarter of its length and full of many rows of teeth. A gulper eel's huge mouth can inflate like a big balloon. This allows it to catch prey much bigger than itself. Gulper eels are also known as pelican eels, as their lower jaw can stretch out just like a pelican's beak can. This creepy eel can grow to up to 2.5 feet long.

LIKE MY TAIL?

The end of the **gulper eel**'s tail can glow a pinkish red and even flash off and on. The gulper eel is not very good at chasing, so its glowing tail attracts prey. Once the unlucky creature is close enough to its mouth, the gulper lunges forward quick as a flash to engulf its prey whole!

SNAP!

3,300 TO 9,900 FEET DEEP

49

LANTERN SHARK

ETMOPTERUS SPINAX

The **lantern shark** is a type of dogfish. It can grow up to 17 inches long and is found throughout the Atlantic Ocean and the Mediterranean Sea. Lantern sharks like to eat small fish, squids and crustaceans.

GLOWING BELLY

Patches on the **lantern shark**'s underside glow a blueish green—these can be seen from up to 13 feet away! Scientists think this helps the shark stay hidden from predators who look up from underneath. Sharks as a group have evolved the ability to make light twice, which means they've found it useful for survival. Light-producing sharks are very successful creatures, as they make up around 12 percent of all shark species.

BYCATCH

Fishing boats often catch fish by trawling, in which a large net is pulled beneath the boat. Unfortunately, the **lantern shark** is often accidentally caught by trawlers; this is called "bycatch." Fishing boats often throw away any bycatch, but sadly by then it is too late for the shark. Because of too much fishing in the Atlantic Ocean, scientists fear that the number of lantern sharks is getting smaller.

EVOLUTION

Life on Earth is not stagnant. The kinds of plants and animals that can be found on our planet change through the millennia. This is known as evolution. If you go back far enough—millions of years—you would look very different from your ancestors. So different, in fact, that you are now a distinct species from them. Why do we change? The answer lies in the world around us. Over long periods of time, environments change and creatures find new places to live. Animals and plants evolve to better suit the conditions they find themselves in. The animals that evolve the most successfully— whether that means they have bigger teeth than their ancestors, or a powerful new light-lure—will find more food and have more babies than the ones that don't.

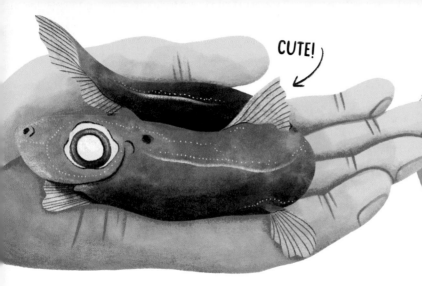

CUTE!

TEENY TINY

There is a dwarf lantern shark, *Etmopterus perryi*, that can fit in the palm of your hand!

ATOLLA JELLYFISH

ATOLLA WYVILLEI

Some deep-sea jellies are as beautiful and surreal as dreams. The **atolla jellyfish** is found in the Midnight Zone all over the world's oceans. It has a red body with 20 long tentacles trailing behind. It also has one extra-special tentacle that is much longer than the others. This tentacle has a glowing lure on the end, which it uses to attract prey.

6 INCHES WIDE!

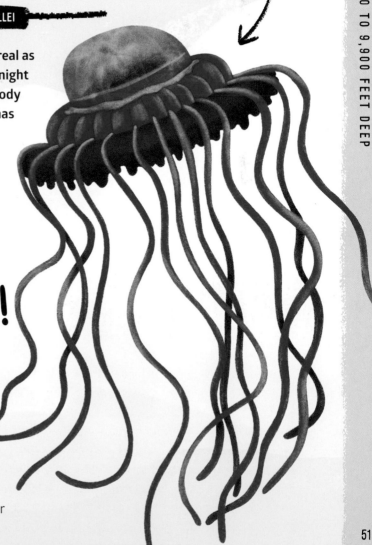

STAY AWAY . . .

OR I'LL SOUND THE ALARM!

You don't want to mess with the **atolla jelly**, or it might set off its light alarm! When the atolla jelly feels threatened it produces a wonderful show with continuous flashes of blue light. These flashing lights can be seen from over 300 feet away. It is thought the jelly uses these lights to attract bigger animals, which will hopefully prey on whatever creature is threatening the jelly.

3,300 TO 9,900 FEET DEEP

51

DEEP-SEA JELLYFISH

DEEPSTARIA ENIGMATICA

What looks like a harmless floating plastic bag is actually . . . a balloon of doom! *Deepstaria enigmatica* is a type of jellyfish. Unlike most jellyfish, its tentacles are all but nonexistent. Its bag-shaped body can reach up to 3 feet across, and it floats along in the deep sea, waiting to bump into an unlucky meal. It was first discovered in the 1960s and lives in the world's oceans at depths of up to 5,750 feet.

OUCH!

Jellyfish are related to sea anemones and corals, and all of these creatures have stinging cells called nematocysts. Jellyfish will often have stinging cells on their tentacles. Although *Deepstaria enigmatica* has no tentacles, scientists think it has stinging cells all over its body.

EVERYONE LIKES JELLY

When they die, the *Deepstaria enigmatica* jellies fall to the bottom of the ocean. Such a large meal attracts masses of scavenging crabs and shrimps, who rush to join the feast! Scientists have been lucky enough to witness one of these jelly falls, using a camera attached to a submarine.

LET ME OUT!

So what does this jelly do when it is lucky enough to come across a tasty treat? It traps its prey inside its large body. It can quickly close its opening, just like you would close a drawstring on a garbage bag. Stinging cells inside its body likely sting the prey to paralyze it. Once the prey is still, little hairs on the inside of the jellyfish move the prey towards its mouth.

I STILL CALL MY JELLY HOME

There is one creature that seems to be protected from **Deepstaria enigmatica**'s balloon of doom, and that is an **isopod**. Isopods are a kind of crustacean with seven pairs of legs and a tough, segmented exoskeleton. (An exoskeleton is a hard skeleton on the *outside* of an animal's body.) This special little isopod sits inside the jellyfish safe and sound, taking bites of whatever the jelly traps. What a good deal for the isopod—free meals and board, and safety from predators! Almost all of these deep-sea jellies have been found to have an isopod living in them.

CUTE!

NARROWNOSE CHIMAERA

HARRIOTTA RALEIGHANA

The **narrownose chimaera** is found in oceans all over the world and lives in waters up to 9,800 feet deep. With its long, pointy nose and tail it can reach up to 4 feet in length. It likes to stay close to the ocean floor and uses its two large eyes to find small crustaceans and shellfish. The narrownose chimaera is also known as a rabbit-fish, but it definitely does not look as cuddly as your pet rabbit!

COSMIC SEA JELLY

BENTHOCODON HYALINUS

Do not get confused: this is not a flying saucer from outer space, it's a jelly from the depths of the ocean! The .8-inch-long **cosmic sea jelly** has been spotted 9,900 feet down in the Pacific Ocean, just off Samoa.

OUTTA THIS WORLD!

UNDERWATER MOUNTAINS

The **cosmic sea jelly** was found by scientists who were hovering by a seamount. A seamount is an underwater island in a mountain range that is formed by volcanoes. Seamounts are known as biodiversity hot spots and are home to a huge number of deep-sea creatures. Water currents surrounding seamounts bring up extra nutrients and food from the sea floor, attracting all sorts of life.

FLANNERY FILE

ORANGE ROUGHY

The **orange roughy**, or deep-sea perch, likes to live in big groups near seamounts. When fishermen discovered them breeding in large groups, they found that they could scoop up a million dollars' worth of fish in one trip. The restaurants of the world were suddenly filled with their succulent fillets. Orange roughy, although just 1 foot long, can live for a century and a half—so old for a fish! There seems something terribly wrong about eating a 150-year-old fish, and as soon as I learned this they disappeared from my dinner plate.

EXPLORER SPOTLIGHT

EXPLORING UNDERWATER MOUNTAINS

The seamounts of the ocean deep are home to an astonishing variety of corals that never see the light of day. Known as black, golden and red corals, these coral forests can reach 200 feet in height, and support as much life as a tropical rainforest! Lots of other animals live in and around these coral forests. Red and white crabs crawl through the corals, as do medusa sea stars, their arms ruffling around restlessly like miniature serpents. When I became a museum director at the Australian Museum in Sydney, I got to hire someone who became a real deep-sea explorer. His name is Greg Rouse. He kept in touch and I was amazed to hear his stories. He told me that one time he went down in a submersible in the South Pacific and became the first human ever to explore an entire mountain range—although this one was sunk 2.5 miles down in the deep! He saw lots of new species, but some, including an octopus, escaped from his net on the way up. He also had a surprise. One morning he reached the ocean bottom 2.5 miles below his research vessel—and discovered a filleted fish lying on the bottom! The kitchen staff had filleted it and thrown the head and spine overboard. It had gone directly down, not drifting at all. The mid-ocean can be a very still place.

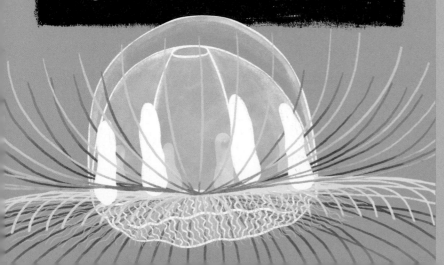

TOO MANY TENTACLES

The **cosmic sea jelly** has two sets of tentacles—one that faces up and one that faces down. There are over 800 tentacles total! Scientists are not sure why this is, though some think all those extra tentacles are useful while hunting. Through its completely see-through body you can see this jelly's bright red digestive system, as well as several glowing yellow blobs. These yellow blobs are organs that the jelly uses to make baby sea jellies!

SEE-THROUGH JELLIES

In a world where there is nowhere to hide, being see-through is a good strategy. This means that many of the creatures of the deep are simply invisible to us, even if they're 3 feet long and sitting at the end of our noses. Sea jellies and other similar creatures specialize in this kind of defense, and they are found everywhere in the deep, truly dominating life there.

PATAGONIAN TOOTHFISH

DISSOSTICHUS ELEGINOIDES

The **Patagonian toothfish** likes the colder waters of the southern hemisphere. Young ones prefer shallow waters, where they eat tiny crustaceans known as krill. As they get bigger and bigger they venture into deeper waters (as far down as 12,600 feet) in search of fish. As adults they are opportunistic predators, meaning they will take a bite out of anything tasty that comes their way!

THEY GROW TO OVER 6.5 FEET IN LENGTH AND LIVE FOR A LONG TIME FOR A FISH—OVER HALF A CENTURY!

WOW!

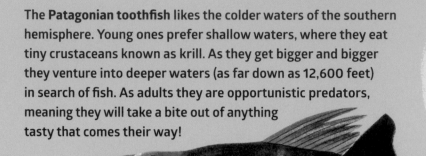

DON'T OVERFISH ME!

Humans fish for the **Patagonian toothfish** in great numbers, as it is considered a luxury seafood in many countries. Unfortunately, it's in danger of being overfished. It is particularly vulnerable as it takes up to nine years to become an adult and make its own babies. Fishing for the Patagonian toothfish is usually done by trawling, in which a big net is towed beneath a boat. Many other fish and marine mammal species can accidentally become caught in the trawling net, too, which can lead to them dying. If you want to help save the Patagonian toothfish, don't fish for it or eat it!

OPERATION ICEFISH

Governments can make rules to protect fish populations, such as where you can fish and how many fish you can take. These rules are important as they make sure certain species do not become endangered. Sometimes fishing boats break these rules and take part in illegal fishing.

During Operation Icefish (2014–2016), one illegal fishing boat called *Thunder* was chased through intense storms, huge waves and around floating ice. *Thunder* was breaking the rules by fishing large numbers of toothfish. It was followed from Antarctica to western Africa by a ship owned by Sea Shepherd, an organization of "eco-warriors." Finally, after a hectic 110-day hunt, Sea Shepherd caught up with *Thunder*—except *Thunder* was sinking and the crew had to be rescued! The captain and chief engineer of *Thunder* were fined 17 million dollars and were also sent to jail.

BLACK SWALLOWER

CHIASMODON NIGER

Although only small, reaching 10 inches, the **black swallower** can devour prey more than ten times its size. It uses its big, toothy mouth to swallow fish whole and is able to digest them in its expanding belly. Its stomach can expand so much that its skin becomes see-through! These balloon-belly fish are found as deep as 8,900 feet in the Atlantic Ocean.

EYES **BIGGER** THAN iTS iNFLATABLE STOMACH

Sometimes the **black swallower** bites off more than it can chew. Some dead black swallowers have been found floating on the surface with exploded bellies! This can happen when the fish swallows prey that is just TOO big. Before it is able to digest the prey, the prey begins to decompose, releasing gases. These gases make the black swallower's belly go . . .

POP!

EVER WISH YOU COULD EXPAND YOUR STOMACH TO FIT IN THAT SECOND SLICE OF BIRTHDAY CAKE? WELL, THE BLACK SWALLOWER CAN—IN FACT, iT COULD FIT iN AN ENTIRE CAKE AND MORE!

3,300 TO 9,900 FEET DEEP

57

PACIFIC VIPERFISH

CHAULIODUS MACOUNI

Viperfish are one of the scariest-looking fish in the depths, and they have a reputation for being ferocious. There are nine species of viperfish and all have large eyes and big fangs. Their fangs are so big that the teeth on their lower jaw rest outside of their skulls, almost poking into their eyes. These shiny, silvery-blue fish live in the Pacific Ocean and get down to a depth of over 13,000 feet, migrating to the surface at night to eat lots of different things, like crustaceans, squids and other fish.

UP TO A FOOT LONG!

VIPERFISH JAIL

It's hard to get food in the deep sea, so animals evolve all sorts of weird and wonderful ways to ensure they get a hold of a meal. The **viperfish** can swim very fast to catch its prey. It uses its long teeth like the bars in a jail cell—once you're in, there is no way of getting out! Their jaws can also unhinge (where the upper and lower jaw dislocate so that they do not connect), allowing it to swallow prey that's larger than it is. One species, the glass-fanged viperfish, has the largest teeth relative to its skull of any fish in the world!

WOW!

NOW YOU SEE ME . . .
NOW YOU DON'T

The **Pacific viperfish** has a glowing belly. It uses this to match the background light of the deep blue sea, helping it to stay well hidden. Some species of viperfish also have a light on the top of their dorsal fin—that's the fin on their back—to attract unsuspecting prey.

GET ME OUT OF HERE!

HEADLESS CHICKEN MONSTER

ENYPNIASTES

Despite being discovered in 1882, this puzzling creature is rarely seen. It has been found as deep as 18,665 feet and was recently captured on video by Australian scientists 9,900 feet down in the Southern Ocean. It has such a weird name because when it first used its unusual fins to swim towards the underwater camera, it reminded scientists of a chicken about to be popped into an oven!

IF IT'S NOT A CHICKEN, THEN WHAT IS IT?

The **headless chicken monster**, believe it or not, is actually a type of sea cucumber. Sea cucumbers are related to sea stars, brittle stars and sea urchins. Its purplish, barrel-shaped body reaches up to 10 inches in length and it has a mass of tentacles surrounding its head. It uses these tentacles to carry bits of sea floor into its mouth. Being a deposit feeder, as most sea cucumbers are, it passes large amounts of sea floor through its digestive system to find and eat lots of tiny bits of hidden food. Then it has to poop out the excess sediment, which forms trails behind it. You can often see where a sea cucumber has been by following its poop trails! The headless chicken monster only spends time on the bottom to feed, using its fins to swim up into the water at other times.

3,300 TO 9,900 FEET DEEP

A GENIUS DEFENSE

This fragile, jelly-like animal needs to protect itself in the vast ocean, and it does this in a most unique way. The **headless chicken monster** can make light within its skin. Its entire body will glow when it is touched. But, even better, when a predator hassles this clever fellow it leaves the scene of the crime painted with spots of the chicken monster's shining skin! This is terrible news for the predator, as it is now a glowing beacon attracting its own predators.

AMAZING!

SQUIDWORM

TEUTHIDODRILUS SAMAE

The **squidworm** is a kind of worm. Instead of burrowing down into the ground, it loves to swim freely above the ocean floor.

IS IT A SQUID OR A WORM?

4 INCHES LONG!

FEEDING TENTACLES

EXPLORER SP🔍TLIGHT

HOW DO SCIENTISTS LEARN ABOUT THE DEEP SEA?

To discover animals of the deep sea, scientists can use a whole host of techniques. They can send down traps—which often look like a big cage with bait in the middle—to collect animals. Or they can attach a video camera to a submarine! Deep-sea submarines with no humans inside them are called remotely operated vehicles, or ROVs. The **squidworm** was discovered by an ROV in 2007, off the coast of Borneo, at almost 9,900 feet deep. Scientists were shocked that such a weird animal could escape our attention for so long. They think that it was good at swimming away from the collecting traps that scientists had set up in the deep ocean. Also, even if it had been found in a trap, its soft body would have been easily damaged on the trip back to the surface. Using a ROV means scientists can observe animals in their natural habitat and learn a lot about their behavior.

HANDY!

FASCINATING FEATURES

The **squidworm**'s body is see-through and it has many tentacles surrounding its head. Two of these tentacles are yellow and curly; it uses these ones to filter water to find scraps of food that have floated down from the surface.

The squidworm uses its other tentacles for breathing and finding its way around in the dark depths. These are extra-special tentacles because they can be stretched out really far— longer than the squidworm itself. Hidden in between its tentacles are two feathery "noses" that it uses to detect chemicals in the water. And down the body of the squidworm are loads of hairy, oar-like limbs. When the worm is swimming, these oars move in unison—a bit like doing the wave!

GIANT JELLYFISH

STYGIOMEDUSA

This **giant jelly** is likely the largest invertebrate predator of the deep sea. (Invertebrates are animals that have no backbone or hard inside skeleton.) The giant jelly has a dark red, bell-shaped body, up to 2.5 feet wide. Attached to its body are four thick arms that dangle up to 20 feet down! These arms are likely used to hold on to prey.

Giant jellyfish have been found in deep oceans all over the world, loving cold water temperatures between 30 degrees Fahrenheit and 40 degrees Fahrenheit. The giant jelly has been spotted in the Gulf of Mexico, at around 6,600 feet deep.

A FISHY FRIEND

Friendships between fish and deep-sea jellies are rare, and are known as symbiotic relationships. The **giant jellyfish** has been seen several times with a much smaller, white fish in tow. Scientists observed this little white fish friend staying close, following the giant jelly wherever it went! Friendships go both ways, and it is likely this little guy gets shelter and food while getting rid of unwanted parasites from the giant jelly. Scientists think that, to protect itself from the jelly's stingers, the little white fish might wear a coat of protective goo. Imagine if you had to wear a layer of slime just to hang out with your friends.

EW!

61

FLABBY WHALEFISH

DITROPICHTHYS STORERI

There are 30 species of **flabby whalefish**, the biggest reaching 15 inches long. These fish have large mouths and their fins are very far down their bodies. They cannot make their own light. Despite this, they are well adapted to living in the Midnight Zone. Below 5,900 feet, there may be more species of whalefish than any other fish. They undergo a nightly trip to shallower waters to find food.

THE FLABBY WHALEFISH IS SO NAMED BECAUSE IT LOOKS A LITTLE LIKE A WHALE, AND HAS LOOSE SKIN AND NO SCALES.

THE PUZZLE OF THE WHALEFISH

The unassuming **whalefish** has been the focus of a big scientific mystery—for over 100 years the males, females and young whalefish were all thought to be different species! Not only is there no family resemblance between them, but they also live out their lives in different ocean zones.

In 1895 the first whalefish was discovered 3,300 feet down and over the years more than 500 individuals were collected. Oddly, they all happened to be female. About fifty years later, scientists discovered a little fish living on the surface. It had an upturned mouth and a long tail, and it was named a tapetail. Over 100 individuals were found and, curiously, they were all very young. Where were all their parents?! Enter the bignose. Like the whalefish, the bignose fish was found living in the deep sea. Scientists found about 65 bignose fish, and they were all male. Coincidence? Think again! Finally, in 2003, scientists figured it all out. What were once thought to be three species—the whalefish, the tapetail and the bignose—were found to be one big happy family! How many more scientific mysteries are awaiting your discovery?

MONOPLACOPHORANS

Monoplacophorans have a single shell with a big gooey foot that they use to suction onto the sea floor. Their shell looks like a little hat sitting on the ground. They can attach to hard or soft ground and are often found near seamounts, just like the **cosmic sea jelly** (see page 54).

Above its fleshy foot is a mouth and lips that it uses to munch on tiny bits of food it finds on the sea floor. These little hat-like creatures move slowly, leaving wavy trails of sea floor dirt behind them. Weirdly, monoplacophorans have multiple sets of kidneys, hearts and gills! It is thought these extra organs may help monoplacophorans breathe better.

.1 TO .3 INCHES LONG

I'M ALIVE!

3,300 TO 9,900 FEET DEEP

Monoplacophorans first became known to scientists as fossils, and were thought to have become extinct 375 million years ago. Live ones were not discovered until the 1950s, when they were dredged up from the ocean floor 11,500 feet down. At the time, it was celebrated as one of the biggest biological discoveries of the century! Now there are over 35 living species known to scientists.

COLOSSAL SQUID

MESONYCHOTEUTHIS HAMILTONI

You may have heard tales of a **giant squid** terrorizing sailors in the ocean far away. But have you heard of the even larger **colossal squid**? The colossal squid is the heaviest invertebrate on Earth. (An invertebrate is an animal without a backbone.) The largest colossal squid ever found weighed in at a whopping 1,100 pounds! That is as heavy as a large horse. This hefty squid loves the cold waters around Antarctica and is found across all of Earth's southern oceans at depths of up to 6,600 feet.

This species was first discovered from digested remains in the stomach of a **sperm whale.**

KiLLER BARREL

The **colossal squid** is a red, muscular beast that can be up to 20 feet long. It has a plump, barrel-shaped body known as a mantle. The mantle ends in two wide fins that are shaped like an arrow, and below them is a head with two eyes the size of dinner plates. To finish things off, it has eight long arms and two even longer feeding tentacles.

A SQUID WITH A BEAK?

The body of a **squid** is almost all soft, except for one important part. Hidden between its tentacles is a mouth surrounded by a very hard beak. The squid uses this powerful beak for killing and ripping apart its prey. It's almost like a killer ocean parrot! Sperm whales and other creatures eat squids, and squids' beaks are often found inside their predators' stomachs. Scientists study these beaks and are able to find out how large the squid was. Some beaks are even bigger than the biggest whole squid ever found. It is likely these squids grow much larger than the record of 1,100 pounds.

WHERE CAN I SEE ONE?

Lucky for you, you don't have to dive into the deep to see a **colossal squid**. You just have to fly to New Zealand! The body of a colossal squid is preserved at the Museum of New Zealand Te Papa Tongarewa. This squid was captured by someone who was fishing in Antarctic waters. Unfortunately, even out in the ocean, humans usually only see colossal squids that have already died. Only twelve whole colossal squids, most of which were accidentally caught by fishing boats, have ever been studied by scientists.

BIRD FOOD

Albatrosses, a type of large seabird, are thought to scavenge these beasts; if they bump into a dead squid, they might take a nibble. Scientists know this because sometimes albatrosses' stomachs contain colossal squid beaks.

ENORMOUS EYES

Along with the **giant squid**, the **colossal squid** has the largest eyes of any animal on the planet. It is thought these oversized squids use their huge eyes to better see their arch nemesis, the sperm whale. The colossal squid is the favorite prey of the sperm whale. Many sperm whales have scars on their bodies from life-and-death struggles with squids.

On each enormous eye, the colossal squid has a light-producing organ called a photophore. Scientists are not certain what the squid does with these eye-torches. One idea is that they help camouflage the squid when it is searching for prey. Maybe in the dark its two eye-lights look like two small, glowing fishes. Another idea is that it can use these lights to better see its prey when it is up close and personal.

3,300 TO 9,900 FEET DEEP

TOP PREDATOR

The **colossal squid** is thought to be the top predator of the Southern Ocean. It is likely an ambush predator. Instead of chasing prey at high speeds, it hides and then attacks them by surprise. It has deadly hooks on its tentacles to catch its prey. Its favorite foods are fish, such as the Patagonian toothfish, sharks and other squid.

I'M READY TO RUMBLE!

MID-OCEAN VENTS

MiD-OCEAN VENT

MAGMA

OCEANIC CRUST

MANTLE

The bottom of the ocean, also known as the sea floor, is not an entirely still and quiet place. In fact, over time whole new bits of sea floor can be created, and when that happens there is lots of activity in the area! Sea floor is also called oceanic crust and it is made deep down in the middle of the ocean. Like a slow-moving conveyer belt, new crust bursts forth from inside the hot Earth. In the area where this new crust is being formed, a type of opening called a mid-ocean vent appears in the ocean floor. It's a bit like an underwater volcano. Here the hot mantle, the layer of the Earth between the molten outer core and the thin crust on top, is closer to the surface. Heat escapes from these mid-ocean vents, causing the surrounding water to become very hot.

Mid-ocean vents can also be called hydrothermal vents, hydrothermal meaning "hot water." Even though the surrounding sea water is around 34 degrees Fahrenheit, water very close to hydrothermal vents can reach over 750 degrees Fahrenheit! This extra-hot sea water does not boil due to the great pressure down here. An assortment of interesting minerals and chemicals escape from these vents. This unusual ocean chemistry allows for a host of strange and unfamiliar animals to live, like giant red-plumed worms, hairy farming crabs and killer sponges!

The mid-ocean vents are an incredibly special place. Animals down here live unlike any other animal on Earth. On the surface of the Earth, plants and some bacteria use sunlight, water and carbon dioxide to make themselves food. This is called photosynthesis. Sunlight and photosynthesis are the basis for almost all life on Earth.

But deep down in the ocean near these vents there is no sunlight. Instead of relying on food drifting down from the zones above, organisms down here have figured out another way to feed themselves. Some bacteria are able to use chemical energy for food; this is called chemosynthesis. These very special bacteria love to snaffle up the chemicals coming out of the vents to make themselves food. The animals living near these vents have developed close relationships with these bacteria, and many have them living on or in their bodies! Some animals down here don't even have mouths or guts, as the bacteria provide them with all the energy they need. Without this close relationship, nothing would be able to live in this hostile environment. Let's have a closer look at some of these amazing creatures!

SQUAT LOBSTER

You may never have heard of a **squat lobster**, but on the sea floor they rule the roost. There are over 900 recognized species, and they live in all sorts of places, from shallow coral reefs to the vents of mid-ocean ridges. Mid-ocean ridges are underwater volcanic mountain ranges, where new ocean floor is being made. Squat lobsters have been found at a depth of 16,400 feet and several species are even happy on land, living in caves close to the ocean. Squat lobsters are so plentiful that every year dozens of new species are discovered or described!

Discovering an animal means finding out about it for the first time. Describing an animal is the next step, when it is studied and formally named.

ZZZZZZ . . .

Squat lobsters do not carry shells like hermit crabs do, so when it's time to sleep, they need to find a safe place to hide from predators. They crawl backwards into crevices or hide under rocks, leaving their sharp claws facing outwards to pinch anyone who might be coming their way!

SNAP!

SIFTING FOR A SNACK

Squat lobsters have ten legs, with the first pair ending in their all-important sharp claws. Most are scavengers, but some prey on small animals in the ocean. The squat lobster scoops up mud and sand from the ocean floor in its powerful claws and then sifts through it until it finds the food it needs. Imagine if you had to eat that way. Mealtimes would take forever!

ALL THE COLORS OF THE RAINBOW

YEAH!

WORK IT!

Squat lobsters come in all shapes and sizes. Some species are long, thin and pointy, like a daddy-long-legs spider. Others are short and fat and have extra-thick exoskeletons, which are skeletons that sit on the outside of a creature's body. There are even some that are covered all over with spikes, zebra stripes or bright red spots. Squat lobsters have differing looks for all sorts of reasons, like protecting themselves, finding food or attracting a mate. These incredibly colorful creatures may look like lobsters, but they are actually related to hermit crabs.

EXPLORER SPOTLIGHT

EXPLORING MID-OCEAN VENTS

In 2011 scientists sent a remotely operated vehicle (ROV), a type of robot submarine, down 9,200 feet to explore animals living near mid-ocean vents. They chose a vent 1,250 miles southeast of Madagascar called Dragon's Breath. They explored an area no bigger than a football field—there is so much life near vents that scientists do not need to explore large areas! Incredibly specialized animals from this area were already known, such as the **hairy-chested crab**. On this single trip scientists discovered six new species, including several weird snails and worms—animals never before seen by humans!

A BACTERIAL COAT

Squat lobsters that live near mid-ocean vents rely on bacteria for energy. The outside of these animals is covered in fine, thread-like epibiotic bacteria. These lobsters must stay within several feet of the hot vents for their entire lives, as the bacteria on their bodies like to stay cozy and warm.

BEST PALS

Epibiotic means one creature is living on the surface of another, causing no harm to its host (unlike a parasite, which does cause harm to its host). Barnacles are epibiotic—sometimes they live on the skin of whales. You may have also seen a suckerfish, called a **remora**, catching a ride with a bigger fish, such as a shark. These are also epibiotic creatures!

YETI CRAB

KIWA HIRSUTA

The **yeti crab** is actually a kind of **squat lobster**. It was first discovered in 2005 on a vent near Easter Island and only five species of this crab have been described since. The average yeti crab is around 6 inches in length and all species discovered have been found in the southern hemisphere.

ME? A MONSTER?

The **yeti crab** was named after the mysterious yeti, the big snow monster that some people believe roams the Himalayan mountains. Just like the mythical yeti, the yeti crab has long, fine hair covering its body, and its claws are very hairy, too.

BACTERIA FARMERS

You've probably heard of dairy farming, or potato farming, but have you heard of bacteria farming? The **yeti crab** grows its own food: the bacteria on its claws! The hairs on its claws are completely covered in a special kind of bacteria. The yeti crab helps get the bacteria food by waving its claws over ocean vents, a bit like a police officer directing traffic. (Yeti crabs better not get too close to the vent, though, as they might be boiled alive. Temperatures can be as high as 750 degrees Fahrenheit!) Then, once the bacteria have grown, the yeti crab eats them. Yum! But can a yeti crab gain all the food it needs from these microscopic bacteria, or does it need additional scavenged snacks? Scientists are still trying to figure this out.

SPONGE

ASBESTOPLUMA

Sponges are a simple kind of creature that stick to the ocean floor. They have no brains, stomachs or hearts. To find food, most sponges use tiny threads to filter large amounts of sea water. By doing this they are able to catch bacteria and tiny organisms in the water.

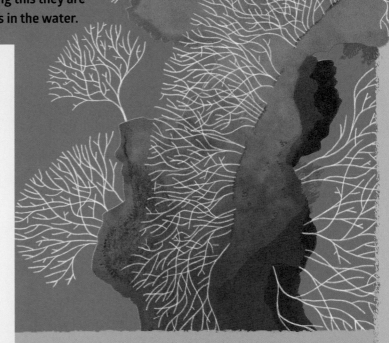

THE QUIET KILLER

As if mid-ocean vent environments were not weird enough, enter the carnivorous sponge! It lives deep in the Pacific Ocean and has been found living close to vents around 3,900 feet deep. Since their discovery over 20 years ago only seven species have been described. One of them is **Asbestopluma monticola**. It stands around 7.5 inches tall with delicate branches extending up into the water column.

COME CLOSER TO MY DEADLY HOOKS

These killer sponges are covered in tiny, hair-like hooks that are used to ensnare prey. Ouch! If a small crustacean accidentally floats too close, it can become caught in these hooks. But if the sponge has no digestive system, how does it eat? By using extracellular digestion, or digestion outside its body! Once the prey is caught, many small sponge cells move onto the unlucky critter and begin to digest it. It can take these cells from eight to ten days to finish eating any large prey. Have you ever taken that long to finish a meal?

HELP! I'M STUCK!

SCALY-FOOT SNAIL

CHRYSOMALLON SQUAMIFERUM

The **scaly-foot snail** was discovered in 2003, at a depth of 9,900 feet in the Indian Ocean. It is known to inhabit just a small area surrounding mid-ocean vents—an area about the size of two soccer fields.

NICE SUIT!

The **scaly-foot snail** really has it covered when it comes to protection. The snail has a suit of armor on both its shell and its single foot. This armor consists of overlapping plates, which help to protect the snail from predators. The armor plates are made of an iron compound that makes the shell and foot tough and strong. The snail even has a beautiful golden color from its metal coating.

COOL!

A HOME AND A MEAL

The **scaly-foot snail** cannot build its shiny armor all on its own—it needs the help of bacteria. That's because the iron chemicals used for its armor are highly toxic. The chemicals come out of the mid-ocean vents, and the snail needs specialized bacteria to help make these chemicals less poisonous. In exchange for helping, these bacteria get to live on the outside of the snail.

The scaly-foot snail has different bacteria living inside of it; these bacteria help it make food. The snail's digestive system is hardly even there as it does not eat like a normal snail, but it does have a huge gland where its bacteria can live, safe and sound.

DEEP-SEA MINING

The sea floor surrounding mid-ocean vents is very rich in metals. Some companies mine the areas around vents to find valuable metals, such as gold and silver. These metals are used to make all sorts of things that are important to humans. During mining, big chunks of the sea floor are brought up to the surface using large buckets or suction pipes. Once at the surface the valuable metals are separated from the dirt.

Deep-sea mining is causing distress to deep-sea creatures, and even possible extinction. The **scaly-foot snail** is only known to live in three small areas near vents in the vast Indian Ocean. Two of these areas are currently leased by mines and mining can greatly disturb the environment. These snails were recently listed as endangered due to human activities. An endangered creature is one that needs our help as it is close to extinction.

BIG-HEARTED CREATURE

The **scaly-foot snail**'s heart is very large. In fact, it has the largest heart in proportion to body size in the entire animal kingdom! This large heart helps with blood and oxygen circulation, as the deep sea is low on oxygen. What a great survival technique!

SNAIL MAGNET

THE IRON IN THE SCALY-FOOT SNAIL'S ARMOR IS MAGNETIC, WHICH MEANS THIS ANIMAL COULD STICK TO YOUR FRIDGE!

73

TUBE WORM
RIFTIA PACHYPTILA

WHY THE RED FACE?

A **tube worm** uses its plume to filter the chemical-rich sea water, but why is it so red? That's because it is full of blood, which is rich in hemoglobin. Hemoglobin is a protein that carries oxygen and it is the same protein found in human blood! The tube worm uses its blood to transport all sorts of important things around its body.

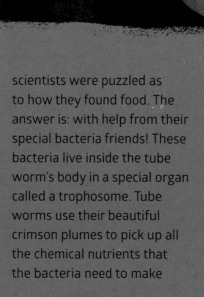

PLUME

DID YOU KNOW?

Animals that can withstand extremely high temperatures, such as those found in mid-ocean vents, are called hyperthermophiles. This means "extreme heat–loving organism."

FIRST OF ITS KIND

At the time of their discovery, tube worms were unlike any deep-sea worms scientists had ever seen. First of all, they had no gut or mouth and scientists were puzzled as to how they found food. The answer is: with help from their special bacteria friends! These bacteria live inside the tube worm's body in a special organ called a trophosome. Tube worms use their beautiful crimson plumes to pick up all the chemical nutrients that the bacteria need to make energy for the tube worm to use. This giant tube worm was the first discovery of an animal getting all the food it needs from the help of special bacteria.

Humans don't have a trophosome, but we do each have a colony of bacteria that help us digest our food. They live inside our gut!

EXPLORER SP🔍TLIGHT

In 1977 a group of geologists took a deep-sea submarine 7,900 feet down to the Galapagos Rift, to explore mid-ocean vents for the first time. The Galapagos Rift is an area where new sea floor is being made, and is located to the west of South America in the Pacific Ocean. Those on the trip expected to find deep-sea volcanoes with no signs of life. Imagine their shock when they came across colonies of giant **tube worms** growing close to the mid-ocean vents!

These tube worms are up to 10 feet in length, each weighing over a pound. Their long white bodies end in a beautiful red plume, which sways in the current as if to say hello. These swaying red plumes sit close together and reminded some people of red roses, leading to one vent site being nicknamed the Rose Garden.

INFECT ME iF YOU CAN!

Even though adult **tube worms** have no mouth or gut, the young worms do. Scientists used to think that bacteria entered the mouths of the young worms and got stuck inside as the worms grew and their mouths and guts disappeared. But recent research suggests that the bacteria actually enter through the skin of the tube worms as they grow, almost like getting an infection.

CLOSE NEIGHBORS

Tube worms live in very dense communities, sometimes upwards of 1,000 individuals per 10 square feet. These tube worm neighborhoods are homes for up to 60 other species. Some of these are crabs and other crustaceans, which nibble at the tube worms' plumes for a meal. Luckily, tube worms are able to draw their plumes into their white, tube-like bodies if a predator comes too close.

DO YOU LIKE YOUR NEIGHBORS? WELL, IMAGINE IF THEY LIVED LESS THAN AN iNCH FROM YOUR FACE!

VENT OCTOPUS

VULCANOCTOPUS HYDROTHERMALIS

There is only one species of octopus that has been found living in mid-ocean vents, and that is *Vulcanoctopus hydrothermalis*, the hot-water volcano octopus. It was found at a depth of 8,500 feet on the East Pacific Rise. The East Pacific Rise, which is off the western coast of South America, is a series of underwater volcanoes where new sea floor is being made.

AT HOME IN THE TUBES

Vent octopuses love to make themselves comfy in the masses of tube worms surrounding mid-ocean vents. When threatened, they can disappear completely into the writhing mass.

THE VENT OCTOPUS IS AROUND 2 INCHES IN SIZE AND LACKS PIGMENT, GIVING IT TRANSLUCENT SKIN.

WALK THIS WAY

Like any other octopus, the **vent octopus** has eight arms, but it uses them in a different way—it likes to crawl on its bottom! Its front four arms slowly move first, followed by the four back arms. Perhaps it moves this way so it can feel where it is going in the darkness? It also uses its tentacles to search for prey. Imagine a sucker-filled tentacle reaching for you in the dark! They aren't all slowpokes, though. When surprised, vent octopuses have been seen shooting off into the distance, taking off like rockets.

Oi!

SEE YA!

YOINK!

DINNERTIME

The **vent octopus** uses its arms to feel around in the dark for its prey. This is called tactile feeding. As well as using touch, noticing changes in pressure and smell also helps it to track down its meals. Not a lot is known about its preferred diet, but it has been seen chowing down on crabs and other crustaceans, such as amphipods.

CONFUSION IN THE DARK?

Scientists do not know much about how **vent octopuses** reproduce, but they have used deep-sea submarines to observe their mating behavior. In 1993 scientists exploring the East Pacific Rise recorded a male vent octopus attempting to mate with another male octopus . . . of a different species!

MAGNIFICENT VENT CLAM

CALYPTOGENA MAGNIFICA

The **magnificent vent clam** is found living around mid-ocean vents in the East Pacific Rise and Galapagos Rift. The clam is a type of bivalve, meaning it is two-shelled, and it is related to oysters and mussels.

SO MUCH BLOOD

The clam needs to find tasty chemicals to feed the pet bacteria living in its gills. It does this by sticking out its siphon into the water (its siphon is a kind of feeding tube). Animals have blood that moves oxygen and nutrients around the body. The **vent clam** uses its blood to move chemicals to feed the bacteria living inside its gills. The clam's blood vessels are so important that they make up almost half of its weight!

CLAMBAKES

When they are young and still in their larvae form, **vent clams** are able to freely swim, but as adults they stay put on the sea floor. The vent clam uses its foot to wedge itself into cracks. Vent clams also love to clump together in groups, and this is known as a clambake!

UP TO 9.5 INCHES LONG!

AN UNCANNY CLAM

This clam is unlike any other clam. First, it has an almost nonexistent digestive system and, second, its gills are home to a colony of friendly bacteria. It also has a red body, as its tissues are full of blood cells containing hemoglobin. Inside hemoglobin, iron and oxygen bind together, and this is what makes blood cells red. These features are common to life near mid-ocean vents.

SHELL OUT FOR INFORMATION

Vent clams are known to live for up to 25 years. How do we know this? Well, the shells of bivalves grow in yearly layers, so all scientists need to do is count them. Trees also grow in yearly layers and scientists often count tree rings to find out their age.

Scientists are also able to use the shells of vent clams to find information about the past. As a vent clam grows, it takes up minerals from the surrounding ocean. These minerals can be used to find out how the temperature of the mid-ocean vent has changed over the time the clam has been alive, as well as the changing chemistry of the ocean!

YUCK!

The friendly bacteria inside **magnificent vent clams** do not just provide food, they also provide protection. When predators come too close, or even try to take a bite, hydrogen sulphide gas is released by the bacteria. Hydrogen sulphide gas smells like stinky rotten eggs. It also makes the clam taste disgusting to predators!

GROSS!

THE ABYSS

The Abyss is a calm and eerie place extending from 9,900 to 19,700 feet deep. It is an area of consistency, where nothing much changes on the seemingly endless ocean floor. Imagine a world with no day or night, and no changing of the seasons. Every day is like the one before. Temperatures are even colder than the Midnight Zone above, with the water close to freezing. The pressure down here is almost 600 times the pressure you would feel on the surface of the ocean, or on land. If you were down this deep you would feel very tightly squeezed from all sides!

Very few creatures can eke out a life in the dark Abyss. The body shapes of those that live here can be quite unusual. Many have no eyes—after all, what is the use of eyes when there is nothing to see? Some have transparent bodies, meaning they have no color, and you can see right through to their insides.

It is even harder to find food down here than it is in the zones above. Most animals rely on little bits of waste raining down from the surface, and predators are less common. Life grows slowly in these dark and cold conditions. In this zone you will find gigantic creatures as well as the world's oldest living animal!

TRIPOD SPIDERFISH AND ABYSSAL SPIDERFISH

BATHYPTEROIS GRALLATOR   BATHYPTEROIS LONGIPES

Abyssal and **tripod spiderfish** are closely related, being some of the deepest living fish. They thrive in depths over 19,700 feet.

A CLEVER BALANCING ACT

SO WEIRD!

The **tripod spiderfish** has a very clever balancing act. It has evolved to use its fins as stilts to perch, motionless, on the ocean floor. Its very long lower fins act as a miniature tripod, and by using them in this way it is able to stand very, very still. Scientists think tripod spiderfish are able to stiffen their fins by pumping extra fluids into them. When they want to swim away again they are able to relax them. They have been spotted on their own or in groups performing their three-legged stand.

BUT WHY HAVE STILTS?

Why would a fish evolve such long, stilt-like fins to be so high above the sea floor? The answer lies in ocean currents and what they bring. An abundance of animals hitch a ride in the ocean currents, such as tasty crustaceans and other fish. But on the sea floor, the currents are much less strong. The higher the **spiderfish** can go on its precarious-looking fins, the more likely it can get a scrumptious meal!

ALL ABOARD FOR A TRIP TO THE SEA FLOOR!

Even though adult **abyssal spiderfish** live in the dark, cold depths of the Abyssal plain, they may remember a time of warmth and sunlight. This is because the little baby larvae of spiderfish begin life in the shallowest parts of the ocean. As they grow, they migrate down and down until they reach the dark and distant sea floor.

COME ON IN!

The fins at the front of the **spiderfish** are also special. Known as the pectoral fins, they are full of sensitive nerves. These fins are held out to the front of their bodies and are able to detect the tiniest movements in the water. Spiderfish use these fins to find and direct tiny crustaceans towards their mouths. Their amazing fins can also detect the vibrations other fish make as they come close to them, helping them sense predators! What a cool superpower!

WOW!

WHY NOT BOTH?

Tripod spiderfish have both male and female reproductive organs. That means they can mate alone or with another tripod spiderfish. The word hermaphrodite is used to describe something living with both male and female sex organs.

9,900 TO 19,700 FEET DEEP

COMMON FANGTOOTH

ANOPLOGASTER CORNUTA

The **fangtooth** is a deep-sea fish with an enormous set of pointy chompers. In fact, it has the biggest teeth relative to body size of any fish! Its teeth are so large that it can never really close its mouth, with the lower teeth sliding into special slots on the inside of its skull instead. Its large head takes up more than a third of its body length. This not-so-cuddly creature is also covered in spiky black scales and has unwelcoming protruding head spines!

FANGING AROUND

The **common fangtooth** is found all over the world, with only two species known to science. The largest fangtooths reach around 6 inches in length. Common fangtooths are a member of the rayfin fish and spend their days safe in the deepest parts of the dark ocean, migrating upward during the night. They do this to find their favorite prey, who often also migrate up to spend the night.

LIKE MOTHER, LIKE DAUGHTER?

Adult and juvenile **fangtooths** look very different from each other, with juveniles not beginning to look like adults until they are half grown. Juveniles have larger eyes and much smaller teeth than their parents. In fact, they look so different that in the early 1800s they were described as two different species!

WAITING FOR FOOD

How does one of the deepest-known fish find its dinner in the pitch-black depths? Mostly, it's luck! These fish patiently wait to bump into prey that they can catch with their giant teeth. Adult **fangtooths** prefer to prey on other fish and squids, whereas young ones catch crustaceans. They aren't fussy with size, either. Fangtooths have been known to catch prey a third of their own size. Once safe in their jaws, the prey is swallowed whole. DELICIOUS!

SEA ANEMONE

STINGING FLOWERS OF THE SEA

Sea anemones are a group of invertebrate animals, meaning they have no backbone. They are the lazy close cousins of jellyfish, lying mostly motionless on the sea floor. They have a cylindrical body ending in a mouth that is surrounded by a billowy collar of tentacles. Some think these creatures look like an ocean flower. Although they may appear pretty and unassuming, their tentacles contain stinging cells, just like the tentacles of jellyfish do. These tiny stinging cells are used to help catch prey. Deep-sea anemones have been known to get quite large—around 1 foot across. They also have weird tentacles with unusually rounded tips.

A VERY ODD HABIT

One of the deepest sea anemones ever discovered enjoys life down at 16,400 feet. This sea anemone, **Losactis vagabunda**, is unlike any of its relatives that live in shallower waters. First of all, this soft, gooey creature can burrow! And not merely a small burrow to escape from predators. It has been seen descending ever so slowly into muddy sediments, and popping out somewhere else many hours later!

To discover more about this very odd sea anemone scientists set up a time-lapse camera on the Porcupine Abyssal plain, off the coast of Western Europe. They were able to take continuous photographs for months, showing how these anemones can move. It is thought this sea anemone developed its burrowing habit to escape from predators and find better spots for a meal. Despite most deep-sea anemones being suspension feeders (meaning they filter tiny bits of food from the water), the scientists also caught footage of L. vagabunda catching a large spiny worm called a polychaete. This polychaete was 15 times the size of the anemone, and it took it an entire day to digest!

9,900 TO 19,700 FEET DEEP

THEY EAT WHAT?!

Some sea anemones, despite being soft and largely motionless invertebrates, are able to catch fast-moving fish! Fish unlucky enough to swim close by and become caught in the tentacles will receive a blast of venom from the stinging cells. Then, while paralyzed, the fish will slowly begin its last trip—towards the sea anemone's open mouth. Unbelievably, the **giant green anemone** has even been found to engulf a baby seabird!

ACORN WORM

ENTEROPNEUSTA

Acorn worms have no eyes, no backbone, and no brain . . . and yet they might be more closely related to humans than they are to garden worms! There are around 111 species of acorn worm, with the largest a whopping 5 feet in length.

COLORFUL CREATURES

Acorn worms were once thought to prefer shallow-water habitats, but by using little submarines that dive very deep down we now know of around 20 species, which come in a huge assortment of shapes and colors. Acorn worms have an acorn shaped "nose" above a collar, followed by a long, wormy body. Their bodies can be yellow, orange, brown, white, pink or purple. Their acorn "nose" can be simple or fancy, with frilly lips!

Shallow-water acorn worms live in U-shaped burrows, poking their heads out to feed. Deep-sea acorn worms have incredibly soft, delicate bodies, making it hard for them to burrow, and most sit atop the sea floor. Unfortunately, their squishy bodies turn into mush when they are dredged to the surface, making it hard to study them!

OH NO!

EVER-CHANGING SCIENCE

Science is how humans figure things out about the world. To discover how animals look and behave, we can use either observation (watching) or experimentation. With more observation and experimentation, scientists are always improving on our knowledge. It is important to remember that scientific knowledge DOES change over time. As we get more and more information, our understanding evolves. Just remember, as you grow up there will always be more to discover about our world!

UP, UP AND AWAY . . . IN MY MUCUS BALLOON!

Acorn worms do not have the ability to swim, but have been observed drifting 65 feet above the sea floor. To do this, they move their bodies in weird ways to create "mucus balloons." They empty their guts of sediment to make themselves lighter. Once they are floating above the sea floor, they are able to use ocean currents to transport them to new areas to find food.

MY COUSIN, THE WORM

Some scientists believe we have some of the same genes as **acorn worms** and that, if we do, we might one day be able to regenerate our bodies like they do. How cool would that be!

POO TRAILS

Acorn worms use their mouths to shovel in sediment from the sea floor. Some species, like the bright purple acorn worm from Hawaii, even have ridiculously large, fleshy lips. These huge lips help them feed on thin layers of especially delicious sediment. Using their long bodies, acorn worms digest organic material and excrete the rest, leaving behind long, winding trails of poo sediment.

YUCK!

9,900 TO 19,700 FEET DEEP

SUPERGIANT AMPHIPOD

ALICELLA GIGANTEA

There are almost 10,000 species of amphipods known to science. Amphipods are little crustaceans that are related to crabs, prawns and lobsters, and they are usually no more than half an inch long. Due to their small size and wide-ranging distribution, they are commonly known as the insects of the sea. Considering this, you can imagine scientists' surprise when several **supergiant amphipods** (some almost a foot long!) were pulled from the depths of the Pacific Ocean in 2011.

MYSTERIOUS CRUSTACEANS

The **supergiant amphipod** was first discovered in 1899, then was not seen again for over 100 years. These secretive creatures are rarely spotted. Why are they so rarely found by scientists? We still do not know.

MAN-EATING CRUSTACEANS?

Supergiant amphipods are known as necrophagous eaters, which means they feed on the decaying corpses of other animals. But if humans were able to swim in the depths of the ocean, would these giant creatures be tempted to have a nibble? In 2017 a boy was swimming at Brighton Beach in Melbourne, Australia, when he was attacked by a swarm of amphipods! His small wounds bled considerably and it was thought the amphipods may have made a substance that stops blood from clotting, just like leeches do. Good news for swimmers is that the scientists at Museum Victoria, who examined the collected specimens, said the attack was unusual amphipod behavior and that the boy likely swum through a feeding group. **OUCH!**

ALBATROSS VOMIT

The largest **supergiant amphipod** ever recorded was over 1 foot long. It was 1983 and on a tropical Hawaiian island, an **albatross** was in trouble. The poor bird had swallowed more than it had bargained for! Heaving and gasping, the bird regurgitated an enormous supergiant amphipod. How do you think the albatross got hold of this giant crustacean—maybe off the corpse of some creature that emerged from the depths? **GROSS!**

SEA SPIDER

COLOSSENDEIS

With a small, thin body and enormously long, pointy legs, *Colossendeis* are a type of sea spider. They are the largest genus of sea spiders, with 72 species. *Colossendeis* can grow to almost 6.5 feet across and commonly prey on comb jellies.

YOU MIGHT THINK YOU'RE SAFE FROM SPIDERS IN THE DEEP OCEAN, BUT THINK AGAIN!

9,900 TO 19,700 FEET DEEP

FLANNERY FILE

RIVER OF LIGHT

Sometimes you can see amazing bioluminescence quite close to big cities. Once, on the Hawkesbury River, I was out at night in a thunderstorm. It was pretty scary. But when it quietened down, the clouds were so dense that there was very little light from the sky. As I drove my boat, the whole river lit up beneath me—tiny animals were making their own light! I saw schools of fish go past, the light in the water even making their eyes glow. A sunken old jetty looked like a ruined underwater city!

COOL!

CAN SOMEONE TURN ON A LIGHT?

When it is pitch-black in the deep ocean but you desperately need a light, what do you do? Make your own, of course! This is called bioluminescence. Many deep-sea organisms are able to make their own light, including *Colossendeis*, jellyfish, fish, worms and sea stars. This internal light switch is useful for all sorts of things, including communication, feeding, attracting mates and protecting against predators.

SEA PIG

SCOTOPLANES GLOBOSA

Do not be fooled by these pinkish, blobby animals. **Sea pigs** are not related to land pigs at all but, astonishingly, are a kind of sea cucumber. They have a unique difference from most sea cucumbers, though—they have legs!

AWWWW! SO CUTE!

THE BABYSITTERS OF THE OCEAN

The Monterey Bay Aquarium Research Institute sent two remotely operated vehicles (ROVs) into the bay off California to observe a very flat area of the ocean with not much life or hiding space. Here they spotted masses of baby king crabs hanging on to the bellies of **sea pigs**! These baby crabs were either hitching a ride or hiding from predators.

FRAGILE NATURE

Sea pigs are quite small compared to land pigs. Only 6 inches long at their biggest— they could fit in the palm of your hand. Sea pigs are really hard to observe as their bodies are so fragile that they will disintegrate if they leave their deep-sea home.

YOU'VE GOT A FRIEND IN ME

Sea pigs hang out together—not because they're playing games or need friends, but because where one sea pig is found, there's bound to be food! Scientists have spotted herds of anywhere from 300 to 600 sea pigs at a time. When they are grouped together they all face the same direction, possibly to take advantage of the current that flows food their way.

THE ROVING COMPOST

Sea pigs are found in every ocean of the world, and use their puffy legs to march across the muddy sea floor in huge numbers. They are scavengers, roaming and ready to vacuum up any organic debris they bump into, including carcasses that float down to the deep.

When sea pigs eat the microbial mud of the sea floor, it passes through their digestive systems and gets pooed out, along with extra oxygen. In this way, they are like a walking compost as they eat and poo, eat and poo all the way across the sea floor. **EW!**

A UNIQUE WAY OF WALKING

Sea pigs have up to six or eight walking legs, which are actually puffed-up tube feet. Tube feet are also found in related sea stars, sea urchins and brittle stars, and are fluid-filled tubes that can be used for moving, eating, sensing or even breathing. These tube feet can be inflated and deflated on demand! The two antennae-like protrusions on top of their heads are also legs. These "head legs" are likely used to help propel the sea pig across the sea floor, or even to help find tasty morsels of food.

BRITTLE STARS

Brittle stars are relatives of sea stars, sea urchins, sea cucumbers and sand dollars. Even though you might be more familiar with sea stars, there are just as many species of brittle stars in the ocean (over 2,000!) as there are species of sea stars. They make themselves at home all over the world, with the majority of species found in the deep sea. Although they look like sea stars, there is one important difference: the way they move.

OH, BABY!

Brittle stars commonly reproduce asexually, by splitting themselves into two halves. These halves can then grow two new brittle stars. That's incredible!

Brittle stars can also reproduce sexually—in most species there are both male and female brittle stars. Some brittle stars keep their babies safe in a chamber in their central disc. This is called brooding, and the babies are kept safe and sound until they are big enough to crawl out! But most brittle stars make new babies by sending their eggs or sperm into the water column—this is called spawning. The floating eggs and sperm join forces to make tiny baby brittle stars.

I'LL HAVE ONE ARM, PLEASE!

As long as the central section of their body is intact, brittle stars can easily regrow lost or damaged body parts. Wow! This is called regeneration.

THREATS

The biggest threats to brittle stars are deep-sea mining and trawling, which disturb the sea floor. They unsettle all the animals that live there, including the brittle stars.

WHAT LONG ARMS YOU HAVE!

One of the largest brittle stars ever discovered had five long arms that were each over 3 feet in length, making it more than 6.5 feet across!

EXPLORER SPOTLIGHT

FIRST ANIMAL DISCOVERED FROM THE DEEP

In 1818 a polar explorer, Sir John Ross, was on expedition in the Arctic in search of the Northwest Passage. Little did he know that while dredging the sea floor, he would come across a **brittle star**—the first animal ever to be discovered from the deep sea. Imagine his shock when all those long, snake-like arms were pulled onboard. He may have thought he had caught a deep-sea monster!

Brittle stars don't have an anus, so they are unable to digest large amounts of sediment to extract food. They have a diverse range of eating habits, though! Some are deposit feeders, scavenging little bits of food off the sea floor. Some species are suspension feeders, using their long arms to catch any food that's floating past. Several species are even deep-sea predators that use smell to find their prey, catching small animals such as crustaceans and sometimes even squids!

wow!

QUITE THE CROWD

Brittle stars often congregate in huge groups, covering thousands of square feet of sea floor. These groups have been known to contain over a million individuals!

FAST MOVERS

Brittle stars use their long, thin legs to push themselves along the sea floor. They move much faster than their sea star relatives, who can only take tiny steps on their tube feet. Some species of brittle star are even known to swim. They use their arms to stroke through the water, just like how you might swim underwater in a pool!

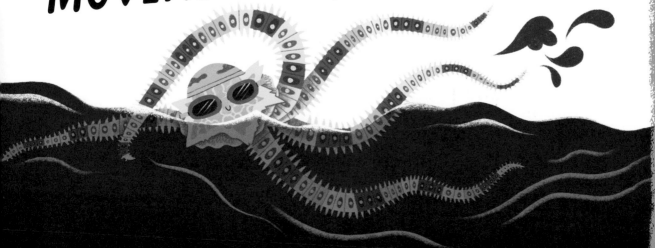

9,900 TO 19,700 FEET DEEP

GHOST OCTOPUS

Is that a ghost I see on the deep-sea floor?! No, it's a brand-new species of octopus! This elusive, transparent octopus was only recently discovered, and is yet to be given a scientific name.

POKING AROUND

Scientists do not know what **ghost octopuses** eat, but they have been seen using their arms to penetrate cracks and nodules on the sea floor. Perhaps they are looking for food?

FAMILY TIES

There are two main kinds of deep-sea octopus. One kind has swimming fins on their heads as well as protruding strands around their suckers, and the other is fin-less and with no strands. The **ghost octopus** has a smooth, bulbous head and belongs to the second group.

TAKING CARE OF BABY

If their appearance isn't creepy enough, these octopuses lay their eggs on the stalks of dead sponges! Down here the temperatures are close to freezing (35 degrees Fahrenheit) and in these conditions it is thought the eggs take years to hatch. **Ghost octopus** parents dutifully stand guard until their eggs are ready to hatch. During this time they never leave the eggs' side, and do not eat at all. They protect their babies from any approaching predators and carefully keep them clean by blowing water bubbles across them. One other species of deep-sea octopus, *Graneledone boreopacifica*, was watched by scientists as it guarded its eggs for four and a half years. What adoring parents!

SO SWEET!

BOO!

GHOSTS
IN THE DEEP PACIFIC

The **ghost octopus** was seen by humans for the first time ever in 2016! It was discovered at a depth of almost 14,100 feet, which is the deepest an octopus of this kind has ever been found. It was spotted by a remotely operated deep-sea submersible, which was exploring the manganese-rich depths of the sea floor off the Hawaiian islands.

FLABBY AND COLORLESS

Octopuses are members of a group of animals known as cephalopods. This group also includes squids and cuttlefish. Many cephalopods have cells in their bodies called chromatophores. These chromatophores contain tiny bits of color called pigments, and are responsible for the rich and vivid colors of many cephalopods. The **ghost octopus** lacks these chromatophores, resulting in its ghostly, transparent appearance.

DEEP-SEA MINING

Manganese is a mineral that forms nodules, or lumps, in some areas of the sea floor. It is mined by humans and is useful in making metals, batteries and even paint. Sea sponges commonly attach to these nodules. Increasing demand for metals such as manganese has resulted in humans mining deep-sea nodules. The removal of these nodules, and the attached sea sponges, is threatening the breeding grounds of the **ghost octopus**.

DEEP-SEA CORALS

Have you ever been lucky enough to go snorkeling on a reef off a tropical island? If so, you might recognize some types of coral. Although they might look like rocks, corals are actually made up of tiny living organisms. Mostly at home in warm water, coral often grow together, building rocky reefs in the photic zone. Most coral need the light because they are in a symbiotic relationship with tiny little sun-loving creatures called **zooxanthellae**. A symbiotic relationship is a close relationship between two creatures, where both creatures benefit from working together. These zooxanthellae live in the coral's hard branches, and use sunlight to make energy. But coral can also be found without zooxanthellae, 6,600 feet deep in the cold, dark waters across the world. These **deep-sea corals** form amazing shapes, including huge fans and columns that stretch far up above.

LONG LIVE THE DEEP-SEA CORAL

Deep-sea corals grow incredibly slowly, sometimes by only a few millimeters a year. This gives them the award for "oldest marine organism on Earth"! In 2009 scientists analyzed Hawaiian deep-water black coral to determine their age. Using carbon dating, they found that the oldest of the corals was 4,270 years old!

PHOTIC ZONE

The top layer of the ocean that receives sunlight is called the photic zone, and is also known as the Sunlit Zone.

A COZY (AND COOL!) HOME

Despite having no **zooxanthellae**, **deep-sea corals** are home to a whole host of other creatures. Lobsters, fish and shellfish all take shelter from currents and predators in corals. Some species of fish even use coral shelter as spawning grounds or as nurseries for their baby fish.

WATCH OUT!

Deep-sea trawling and oil and gas exploration can have a huge impact on corals. Corals live attached to the sea floor, and trawling and mining can destroy their homes. As they are such slow-growing animals, it can take damaged coral hundreds of years to regenerate. Some **deep-sea coral** is collected for use as jewelry, threatening the stability of some populations.

CLIMATE CHANGE AND CORAL

Rising temperatures due to climate change are a great threat to corals. The climate is becoming warmer due to extra carbon dioxide being released into the air. Carbon dioxide from the air gets into the oceans, where chemical reactions turn some of it into an acid. This is called ocean acidification. Corals use a building block called calcium carbonate to make their skeletons. But acid in the sea water destroys calcium carbonate, so it is harder for corals to make their skeletons. It is not just the corals to be concerned about—what about all the animals that call a coral home?

WHALE
— AND —
SHIP FALLS

Dead whales and ships do not seem like the tastiest of meals, but you must remember that food is hard to come by in the deep sea. Nothing down here is wasted. Animals evolve unique ways to thrive in the strangest habitats; if there is an opportunity, it is taken. There are more dead whales lying at the bottom of the ocean than you might think—about 3 million—and there are triple the number of sunken ships, also known as ship falls. Whales and ship falls form a scrumptious smorgasbord for the animals who live down here, who travel great distances to reach this delicious scene of decay.

A dead whale that has sunk to the bottom of the ocean can feed animals for decades, creating its very own ecosystem. There are several stages of the "whale buffet," each welcoming a different specialized animal to the table. The first visitors are the fast and mobile ones: sharks, hagfish and giant isopods. These animals have no trouble stripping the whale carcass down to its skeleton. Not far behind are the little creatures. Tiny bacteria, crustaceans and worms sift through the sea floor surrounding the corpse, seeking any tasty morsels of food. Once the bare bones are exposed, the creepy bone-eating worms appear. Despite having no mouth or stomach, they dig in and feast away. You will have to read on to find out how! Finally, once the bone worms are full, the little sea anemones move on in and attach themselves to the well-worn bones.

Ship falls can also be scenes of astonishing activity. Sunken ships can act as reefs in the deep sea, their hard structures providing safe homes or surfaces to grow on for many creatures. Ships can also provide food for some animals. In this section you will meet the shipworm, a weird creature that has evolved to eat the most unlikely of deep-sea food—wood!

Whale and ship falls are some of the most unusual ecosystems on Earth, being home to a host of weird and wonderful deep-sea creatures.

BONEWORM

OSEDAX PRIAPUS

You might have seen wriggly worms in your garden. They are super important to our ecosystem because they break down organic matter and add nutrients to our soil. But does a similar type of worm exist in the ocean? Yes!

In 2002 scientists discovered a new species of sea creature called the **boneworm**. Yep, they called it a "boneworm" even though it doesn't have any actual bones! These creepy worms were first found feasting on a whale carcass at 9,900 feet depth. For their scientific name, scientists decided to call them *Osedax*, meaning "bone-eating" in Latin. Much like their land-based counterparts, these worms are great recyclers—they help to make compost out of old whale bones.

Boneworms have tube-like bodies ending in stunning plumes that look like ostrich feathers waving in the water. These plumes are actually gills and are used to extract oxygen from their surrounds. Boneworms are related to another weird worm that inhabits deep-sea vents (see **tube worms**, page 74).

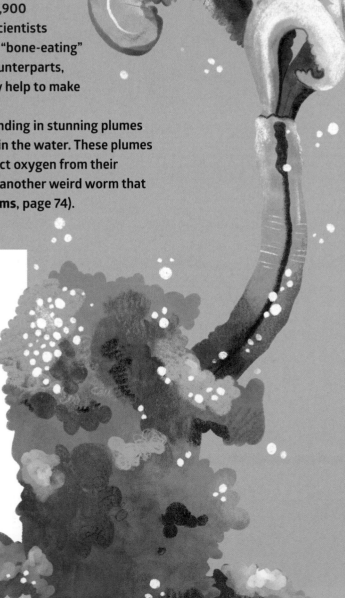

GETTIN' ALONG

A symbiotic relationship is an interaction between two different species, where both help each other out in some way—like **boneworms** and their bacteria.

RECYCLERS OF THE DEEP

Boneworms play an important role—all their bone-munching allows for the cycling of nutrients into the neighboring deep-ocean ecosystem. This makes food aplenty for all the other animals that live down here!

FLANNERY FILE

IN THE NAME OF SCIENCE!

If you are a **boneworm** researcher, it's hard to just wait around until you come across a whale carcass. So to learn more about these weird worms, scientists sometimes sink dead whales, along with cameras, to observe the feast of bones. Scientists discover many new species this way.

I have been able to study many whale bones and skeletons, finding them either in my adventures around the world or hidden away in museum collections. But I have never been lucky enough to see a boneworm in real life!

WOOF!

R

·R·E·X·

WHAT TEENY-TINY BODIES YOU HAVE!

Did you know that there are many more male **boneworms** than females? This is because male boneworms are miniaturized versions of the females and live in colonies in the bodies of larger females. In some species they are up to 100,000 times smaller than the females. In humans, this would mean your dad would fit onto half of a teaspoon! There have been found to be upwards of 100 males living in the tube of any one female. The males never really grow up properly. They would not be able to survive in the big wide world outside the shelter of their females.

EXTRAORDINARY EATING

Boneworms burrow into the bones of whale skeletons to feast on the fats found inside. But boneworms have no stomach and no mouth—in fact, they have no digestive system at all! So how do they eat? The answer is their incredible partnership with bacteria. These bacteria do all of the digesting, cooking up a bone soup for the wormy host. Even weirder, the helpful bacteria live within the "roots" of the boneworms. These roots sprout out of the bottom of the boneworm and help it attach to the whale bones beneath. The roots penetrate deep into the bones so that digestion can begin. Amazing, huh? You can see why scientists were so excited to find these fascinating wriggly creatures. Since 2002, scientists have discovered over 20 species.

101

SHIPWORM

TEREDINIDAE

The **shipworm** is not actually a worm at all, but a bivalve mollusc. This means they have a shell made of two parts and, believe it or not, are related to animals like oysters and mussels. The body of the shipworm is so large—up to 6 feet long—that it couldn't fit into its shell if it tried! Shipworms live in oceans all around the world, in shallow waters as well as the deep open ocean.

A TOUGH MEAL

Wood is not the tastiest of foods and it is also not the easiest to digest. Unsurprisingly, **shipworms** need a little help to gain nutrients from wood. This help comes from a unique type of bacteria living inside the shipworm's gills. These little helpers break down the wood for the shipworms to eat.

DID YOU KNOW?

Even humans get help with digestion from microbes, with over 1,000 species living in our gut!

WORMING THEIR WAY AROUND THE WORLD

There are around 65 species of **shipworm** known to science, many with different ways of living and reproduction. Wood is not that common in the open ocean, so if you come across, say, a sunken ship, it's likely you'll also come across a dense and diverse community of many species of shipworm. The shipworms eat the wood and also use it for shelter. With so many shipworms burrowing down, it doesn't take long before a shipwreck is completely chewed up. Luckily, shipworms are rapid breeders and are able to send their larvae far, far away in search of more floating or sunken wood. These little guys swim and drift along in the water, hoping to bump into something hard. Before they settle down they look for chemicals that let them know if they have found a woody home.

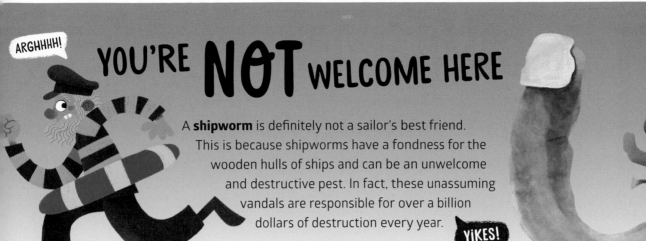

ARGHHHH!

YOU'RE NOT WELCOME HERE

A **shipworm** is definitely not a sailor's best friend. This is because shipworms have a fondness for the wooden hulls of ships and can be an unwelcome and destructive pest. In fact, these unassuming vandals are responsible for over a billion dollars of destruction every year.

YIKES!

A SPECIALIZED SHELL

The shell of a **shipworm** is right at the head-end of its very long body. But instead of using its shell for protection, like many other bivalves do, it uses it during feeding. The shell of a shipworm has teeth-like ridges on its surface, helping it act as a set of chompers to gnaw and burrow through wood.

EXPLORER SPOTLIGHT

A SCOURGE THROUGHOUT HISTORY

Christopher Columbus, an Italian explorer, lost several ships to **shipworms** in 1504. He and his crew staggered back to shore in boats riddled with holes—so many holes that his ship looked like a giant honeycomb! Even thousands of years ago, the Romans applied coats of tar to their ships as protection against the worms.

WOOD YOU LIKE TO EAT?

Shipworms love to munch on one thing: wood. Does it seem odd to you that a sea creature feasts on wood when trees grow on land? Shipworms need wood not only to eat, but to complete their life cycle. So where does all this wood come from? Coastal wood can drift out to sea, with storms causing even the largest trees to become dislodged. This wood eventually becomes waterlogged and sinks to the bottom of the ocean, ready to be latched on to by a shipworm. Shipwrecks are a big favorite of these wormy guys, but they're even happy to nibble on things like floating coconuts. Why did this creature evolve to eat wood? The only answer is: because it could! Animals and plants never lose an opportunity to make a life where others cannot.

103

GIANT ISOPOD

BATHYNOMUS SPP

Have you ever been playing outside and overturned a rock or log, only to find masses of roly-poly bugs? Also known as slaters, these little land crustaceans are actually a type of isopod. They have a much larger deep-sea cousin, the **giant isopod**, which is found in the Atlantic Ocean, Pacific Ocean and Indian Ocean.

The giant isopod reaches up to 2.5 feet long and is known to live in waters over 8,200 feet deep. These big fellows are mostly scavengers. They scuttle along the dark, cold sea floor, waiting patiently for tasty morsels of crab and worm to fall down from above. Every now and then they are lucky enough to come across a dead whale—the dream meal! Some whale carcasses have been seen with huge numbers of giant isopods on them, gorging themselves in unison.

BALL OR BUG?

When it senses danger, the **giant isopod** can roll itself up in a ball to protect itself.

TO THE BRIM

Giant isopods can survive for long periods with no food. When they do eat, they often gorge themselves. After all, they may not come across a huge whale carcass very often! Some isopods have been seen to stuff themselves so much that they have trouble moving after they've finished their meal!

BIG EGGS

Isopods reproduce by laying eggs. The female has a pouch where she can store up to 30 eggs at a time while waiting for them to hatch. Scientists believe they carry one of the largest eggs of all marine invertebrates—up to half an inch long.

ALL THE BETTER TO FEEL YOU WITH

Giant isopods have large eyes to help them see better in the deep ocean. They have also evolved lengthy antennae, almost half the size of their body, to help them feel their way around as they search for food.

VENUS FLYTRAP ANEMONE

ACTINOSCYPHIA SP.

The **Venus flytrap anemone** is a deep-sea anemone that has been found attached to shipwrecks in the Gulf of Mexico. It has also been found in the north and east Atlantic Ocean. This beautiful, orange-colored anemone secures itself to the sea floor, or a sunken ship, with its body and tentacles waving in the water. Its body looks much like a Venus flytrap, a carnivorous plant that eats insects! Just like a Venus flytrap plant closes itself, this anemone closes its two rows of tentacles to trap food inside. The Venus flytrap anemone has been found growing on the weirdest of shipwreck items. It has attached itself to an old gun and even an ancient chamber pot. A chamber pot was used as a toilet in the olden days!

SNAP! SNAP!

HAGFISH

MYXINI

What has three hearts, half a brain, no jaw or backbone, and four rows of teeth on its tongue? A **hagfish**! With their long, smooth and slimy bodies, hagfish are just plain bizarre. They range in size from one and a half to 50 inches and are found in waters worldwide, from the Pacific Ocean and Atlantic Ocean to the Gulf of Mexico and the Mediterranean Sea.

ARE YOU HUNGRY YET?

Hagfish have an incredibly slow metabolism and can go almost seven months without eating a thing.

TO CHEW OR NOT TO CHEW

A **hagfish** is able to sit inside a decaying corpse and absorb nutrients through its skin and gills.

PARTICULARLY PECULIAR

There are 76 species of **hagfish** and throughout history scientists have been stumped about where to place them on the tree of life.

Animals can be separated into two main groups, vertebrates and invertebrates.

▶ Vertebrates have a backbone and skeleton inside their bodies—for example, humans, dogs, whales and fish.

▶ Invertebrates have no backbone and sometimes have no hard parts at all, like a worm or jellyfish.

(Some invertebrates have a skeleton on the outside of their bodies, like beetles and crabs, or a shell for protection, like snails and oysters.)

Are hagfish true vertebrates, even though they have no backbone? Or do they deserve

to be in their own group of animals, somewhere in between invertebrates and vertebrates? As scientists undertake more research it has become clearer that these weird creatures are likely a special kind of primitive vertebrate. A primitive creature is one that has the physical features of its ancestors that lived long ago.

SLIME, SLIME AND MORE SLIME

Hagfish are famous for producing huge amounts of mucusy slime when they are under threat. This slime is incredibly soft and, once released, a teaspoon of the stuff expands 10,000 times—enough to fill a large bucket! Hagfish use their slime to clog up the gills of any fish that dares to come too close. The slime is so extensive that even hagfish can choke on it. If they do become overwhelmed by their own slime, they are able to sneeze it out of their nostrils. To avoid slime flowing onto their faces, they sometimes tie their tubular bodies into a knot to act as a barrier.

THE MOST GOOEY ACCIDENT

In 2007 a truck moving thousands of live **hagfish** crashed on a highway in America. The big jolt surprised the poor hagfish inside, and they released masses of slime all over the road. So much slime was made that several unlucky cars were completely covered in it. Slime was absolutely everywhere! Imagine escaping from your car through a curtain of mucus. **EW!**

FOSSIL HAGFISH

In 300 million years, not much has changed for this creature. The only known fossil **hagfish** is very similar to the modern-day hagfish.

LET'S PARTY!

World Hagfish Day is celebrated on the third Wednesday of October. When this day rolls around, remember to find the beauty in ugly, and care for all animals, especially the ugly ones!

I CAN SENSE YOU

Hagfish are almost blind, but who needs eyes when you have special sensory tentacles? These tentacles surround the hagfish's mouth and are used to feel for food. Hagfish also use their sense of smell to seek out corpses or to prey on live worms. Once they have found their meal—sometimes a dead whale—they will delve in deep and use their tongue-teeth to rip off chunks of flesh. I know who won't be invited to my next dinner party!

SEA ANEMONE

ANTHOSACTIS PEARSEAE

In 2002 a **sea anemone** was discovered with a very odd home; it was living 9,900 feet deep, inside the carcass of a whale near Monterey, California. *Anthosactis pearseae* has yet to be given a common name, and it is only known from this single location. This little anemone is short and stout, white to light pink in color, with flowing stubby tentacles. It almost resembles a molar tooth! It was found stuck on some whale bones, and since no more have been found in the world's oceans, it is thought this may be its preferred habitat.

SO MUCH STILL TO DISCOVER!

WHAT WILL MY NAME BE?

RATFISH

HYDROLAGUS

RATFISH HAVE A LARGE BOXY HEAD AND A BODY THAT ENDS IN A RAT-LIKE TAIL. THEY HAVE TWO BIG EYES AND CAN REACH UP TO 2 FEET IN LENGTH.

Ratfish are closely related to sharks and have a skeleton made of soft and flexible cartilage, just like your nose.

They like to live close to the sea floor, being mainly predators that swim slowly along the bottom, seeking out worms and clams to munch on. They have also been known to cannibalize other ratfish! If they happen to come across a sunken whale carcass, however, they just can't resist the yummy taste of rotting flesh.

Ratfish use both smell and electroreception to find a meal. Electroreception is an amazing kind of super-sense. When animals move, they send out electrical signals. Some animals can detect these signals with special sensors on their bodies. Electroreception is mostly found in animals that live in water, as electricity can travel better in water than in air. Electroreception is used not only to find prey, but to avoid predators and even find a mate.

NIFTY!

THREATS
TO WHALE-FALL ECOSYSTEMS

Because whaling has reduced the number of whales to a sixth of what it once was, the increasing rarity of whale carcasses in the deep sea may have already led to the extinction of some of the specialized creatures that feed on their bones.

TRENCHES

———

The ocean's trenches are the world's most under-explored ecosystem. This is because they are just so hard to get to, and the pressures down here are the most any animal will ever experience. The trenches are also known as the hadal zone, and this zone contains the very deepest parts of the ocean—from 19,700 to an astonishing 35,850 feet deep. To help you understand how deep this is, the tallest skyscraper on Earth is a little over 2,700 feet and Mount Everest reaches just 29,032 feet high!

The ocean's trenches are long and narrow. This is where the oldest and coldest sea floor is recycled back down into the Earth. Just as new sea floor is born at mid-ocean vents, it dies in the ocean's trenches.

The pressure is so great down here that it is very hard for scientists to visit. Scientists can send nets far, far down to catch creatures on the distant bottom. But creatures that live this deep down are usually soft-bodied and very delicate, such as cucumbers and jellies, and they cannot easily handle the journey to the surface. By the time the animal is hauled miles up to the surface, they are often unrecognizable. It is so hard to study life down here that some animals discovered in this zone are known from a single individual specimen. There is still so much to find out about how animals live in the trenches.

In the past few decades humans have been able to send down small submarines to video deep-sea creatures. This has allowed scientists to discover weird and wonderful new species, as well as watch how animals behave. These submarines can be robots, known as ROVs (remotely operated vehicles), or they can have adventurous people squished inside. These explorers are passionate about investigating uncharted territory, no matter how scary! Imagine seeing a deep-sea creature that no one else in the world knows exists. One of these deep-sea explorers is a movie director, James Cameron, who made films such as _Titanic_ and _The Terminator_. Another explorer is Victor Vescovo, an American businessman who holds the record for travelling to the deepest point any human has ever reached!

HADAL SNAILFISH

PSEUDOLIPARIS AMBLYSTOMOPSIS

The **hadal snailfish** holds a big claim to fame: it is the deepest fish ever caught and brought up to the surface to study! The hadal snailfish has been found to live over 26,450 feet down. It's an odd-looking fellow—fish sure look different this deep down. Gone are the scales and giant teeth common to many fish in the Abyssal Zone. Instead, this fish has a pink, slippery, jelly-like body. The hadal snailfish has a very soft skeleton and a skull that is partially open; both of these adaptations are useful for the intense deep-sea pressure.

SURPRISE!

Prior to 2008, the **hadal snailfish** had yet to be seen alive in its natural environment. Scientists only had shrivelled-up pickled specimens to study. When they did spot a live hadal snailfish, it was incredibly active, feeding and swimming around a deep-sea camera. Scientists were really surprised by this—everyone had expected the fish to be very slow and solitary due to the ocean pressure at that depth. Scientists are still learning about how the hadal snailfish is so lively at these pressures.

WHAT IS THERE TO EAT DOWN THERE?

Scientists have had a good look at the stomach contents of some **hadal snailfish** collected from the deep, and found they have not been going hungry. Their tummies were jam-packed with tiny crustaceans! They were all rolled up like macaroni, and looked like the kind of critters you might find in the garden.

HOW EMBARRASSING!

The **hadal snailfish** is so translucent that you can see its organs through its skin!

X-RAY

SEVERAL OF THE WORLD'S
DEEPEST TRENCHES

TRENCH	LOCATION	DEPTH (FEET)
MARIANA *(the deepest trench in the world!)*	Western Pacific Ocean, near the island of Guam	35,850
TONGA	Southwest Pacific Ocean, between New Zealand and Tonga	34,433
PHILIPPINE	Western Pacific Ocean, to the east of the Philippines	32,995
IZU-OGASAWARA	Western Pacific Ocean, stretching south from Japan	32,087
PUERTO RICO *(the deepest trench in the Atlantic Ocean!)*	The border of the Atlantic Ocean and the Caribbean Sea, near the island of Puerto Rico	28,232
SOUTH SANDWICH	South Atlantic Ocean, near the South Sandwich Islands	27,313
PERU-CHILE	Eastern Pacific Ocean, along the coast of South America	26,804
JAPAN	Western Pacific Ocean, along the eastern coast of Japan	26,673
ALEUTIAN	The North Pacific Ocean, along the southern coastline of Alaska towards Russia	26,604

19,700 TO 35,850 FEET DEEP

LIVING UNDER EXTREME PRESSURE

Along with the pitch-black and freezing temperatures, life in the trenches comes with a lot of pressure. Imagine balancing the Eiffel Tower on top of your head: that's how much pressure creatures are under in deep-ocean trenches! If you were down this deep, you would be squished flat as a pancake.

ABYSSAL SEA CUCUMBER

PROTOTROCHUS BRUUNI

Sea cucumbers are a diverse group of organisms, with 1,250 described species. Many of these live in the deep sea. In fact, sea cucumbers can make up more than 95 percent of all of the creatures down here! These soft, vegetable-like organisms are also commonly found in the hadal zone.

STOP, OR I'LL SHOOT!

Sea cucumbers possess another interesting defensive technique. When they feel frightened, they are able to vomit out sticky threads to encase their unlucky enemy. These threads can expand to 20 times their usual size and can be a real pickle to remove. If it's really annoyed, the slippery sea cucumber can even shoot its insides out of its butt! And then it can easily regrow its internal organs when the danger has passed.

BUTT BREATHERS

Sea cucumbers have bucked the trend and evolved to breathe through their anus. Their "lungs" branch out of their backside! Some sea cucumbers also have particularly roomy bottoms—they are so spacious that other fish try to gain entry to make the space their home. No one wants a fish living up their bottom, so some species have evolved anal teeth to keep the unwanted guests out!

DANCERS IN THE DEEP

Most sea cucumbers enjoy a quiet life, slowly plodding along the muddy sea floor ingesting huge amounts of sediment. But for a long time, scientists suspected some deep-sea cucumbers were secret acrobatic swimmers. One such creature, with several body features suitable for swimming, was first hauled aboard a vessel in 1894. But it was not until 2017 that one of these grand gymnasts was caught on camera mid-tumble. *Pelagothuria natatrix* is the world's only known full-time swimming sea cucumber. The footage is incredible. The beautiful *P. natatrix* has a slender purple body ending in a glorious delicate umbrella. It uses this umbrella to pulsate rhythmically, just like a jellyfish.

MEET THE GUMMY SQUIRREL

The **gummy squirrel** is a deep-sea cucumber so named for its thick, tail-like appendage that it holds upright—just like a squirrel does. This creature can grow up to 32 inches long and uses its huge lips to feed. Its "tail" may be used as a kind of sail to help it bounce along the sea floor.

DEEPEST FISH

ABYSSOBROTULA GALATHEAE

With its swollen snout and tiny eyes, *A. galatheae* holds the record for the deepest-living fish ever found. A species of cusk eel, it was found in 1970 at a depth of 27,460 feet in the Puerto Rico Trench.

SAFETY IN NUMBERS

Little is known about **A. galatheae**, but it is thought they breed in a similar way to other cusk eels. These animals release their eggs in a large mass of jelly goo, and send the package floating on its way. **BYE!**

HOW LOW CAN YOU GO?

The **abyssal sea cucumber** has been recorded at 35,062 feet down—the deepest a creature of this kind has ever been found! Rather than crawling along the sea floor scoffing down sediment, sea cucumbers in the Mariana Trench specialize in filter feeding. Filter feeding is where the animal filters large amounts of water to find any tiny bits of food that are floating about. They have specialized tube feet that surround their mouths, and they stretch these out into the current to catch their day's fill. Tube feet are fluid-filled tubes that can be used for moving, eating, sensing or even breathing.

19,700 TO 35,850 FEET DEEP

THE LARGEST EVER FOUND WAS AROUND 6 INCHES LONG.

ALUMINUM AMPHIPOD

HIRONDELLEA GIGAS

Most crustaceans cannot handle depths of more than 14,800 feet. Aside from the extreme pressures, the increased acidity of the water deep down causes their bodies to dissolve. There is only one amphipod that can survive at such great depths, and that's the **aluminum amphipod**. The aluminum amphipod is found as deep as 32,800 feet in many of the world's trenches, including the Mariana Trench, Philippine Trench, Izu-Ogasawara Trench and Japan Trench.

SMALL SPECIMENS

Some amphipods can be very little—the ones collected from the Challenger Deep were only an inch long.

TOUGH AS NAILS

We've met the **supergiant amphipod** (see page 88), but not an amphipod covered in a real aluminum suit of armor! This guy is as tough as nails, having been found at the bottom of the Challenger Deep, the deepest known point on the ocean floor. Aluminum isn't found easily in deep-sea water, but sediments on the sea floor are rich with it. The **aluminum amphipod** swallows these sediments so it can get the aluminum that is needed for its impenetrable suit. What amazing lengths creatures go to in order to survive the world's harshest habitats!

AWESOME ADAPTATION

Adaptation means that you change your appearance or behavior to suit your environment. The **aluminum amphipod** has done just that. Imagine if you could eat bits of metal off the ground and turn those scraps into a full suit of armor!

COOL!

116

BASKET STARS

Basket stars are chaotic-looking creatures, with masses of twirling and clumped arms. Their arms can be up to 3 feet long, with extensive branching and sharp hooks attached that they use to catch their prey. Once their prey is caught in their basket of limbs, they use their arms to carefully place it in their cavernous mouth. Basket stars are actually a type of brittle star, just with extra-fancy and abundant limbs.

DEEP-SEA MONSTER

In 2016, an exploration of the Mariana Trench found a rare type of basket star called a **gorgonocephalid**. These basket stars are named after the gorgons, a type of monster from Greek mythology who had live snakes instead of hair!

ARE WE TRASHING THE FINAL FRONTIER?

While the deep ocean is almost entirely unexplored, it is not untouched. Humans have been bombarding it with an array of materials ranging from deadly toxins to entire ships. Ships can be lost to the sea during war or peacetime. A great many go down with their cargoes and polluting fuel aboard. Even worse, until 1972 it was common practice to dump unwanted weapons at sea, including chemical weapons. Britain alone has dumped 137,000 tons of unwanted chemical weapons at sea and some of the chemicals still remain on the bottom.

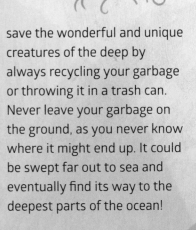

NO PLASTIC, PLEASE!

Plastic debris is one of the most significant threats to biodiversity in the deep ocean, with plastics commonly found in sea floor dirt deeper than 19,700 feet.

Pollutants are chemicals that can harm the environment. They can come from many different sources, including plastics. Pollutants from human activities can also collect in the deepest trenches. Scientists tested amphipods from the Mariana Trench and found they contained over 50 times more pollutants in their bodies than similar animals that live in the most polluted river in China. You can help save the wonderful and unique creatures of the deep by always recycling your garbage or throwing it in a trash can. Never leave your garbage on the ground, as you never know where it might end up. It could be swept far out to sea and eventually find its way to the deepest parts of the ocean!

INDEX

GLOSSARY

AMPHIBIAN

Amphibians are small vertebrates that live in a wet environment. Amphibians include frogs and salamanders.

BACTERIA

Bacteria are microscopic single-celled organisms. They can be found in many different places: in the soil, air and water, as well as on and inside plants and animals—including humans. Some bacteria are beneficial to us, whereas others are destructive.

BIODIVERSITY

Biodiversity is the variety of plant and animal life in a particular habitat, such as one area of the ocean. A high level of biodiversity can help make an ecosystem more sustainable. For example, having lots of different animal and plant life ensures there is enough food to eat.

BIOLUMINESCENCE

Bioluminescence is the production of light by a living organism. This glowing light is created by chemical reactions inside animals' bodies, and can be helpful in many different ways, from scaring off predators to finding food or a mate.

BLOOD CELLS

Blood is made up of blood cells, plus a liquid element called plasma. There are three kinds of blood cells: 1. red blood cells absorb oxygen from the lungs and transport it around the body, 2. white blood cells fight against disease and infection, 3. platelets help to clot blood and heal wounds.

CARBON

Carbon is a chemical element. It is one of the building blocks that plants and animals are made from, making it essential to all life on earth. All organic compounds are considered "carbon-based." Carbon can combine with other elements to make new compounds.

CARBON DIOXIDE

Carbon dioxide is a compound made up of one carbon atom (C) and two oxygen atoms (O_2). It is a greenhouse gas, which means it traps the sun's heat close to the Earth instead of allowing it to move out into space. Too much carbon dioxide causes the Earth to overheat and, as the weather changes, many plants and animals are negatively affected. This is called global warming, or climate change.

CHALLENGER DEEP

The Challenger Deep is the deepest known point on the ocean floor. It has a depth of about 35,850 feet and is located in the western Pacific Ocean.

COLONY

In relation to the scientific study of animals, a colony is a group of animals or plants of the same kind that live together, and often rely on each other to survive.

CRUSTACEANS

Crustaceans are a diverse group of invertebrate animals. All crustaceans have antennae and a tough exoskeleton. Crustaceans include such animals as shrimps, crabs, lobsters, crayfish and krill. All crustaceans originally came from the sea, but some (such as slaters) have adapted to live on land.

CURRENTS

Ocean currents are sections of water that constantly flow in a particular direction. Some currents run along the surface of the water, while others run through the ocean's depths. Currents are affected by the wind, the Earth's rotation, the temperature, differences in salinity (salt content of the water) and the gravitational pull of the moon.

DEPOSIT FEEDERS

A deposit feeder is an aquatic animal that eats little bits of food from the sea floor. Sea cucumbers are deposit feeders.

DESCRIBED SPECIES

A described species is one that has been newly discovered and written about in a scientific paper. A formal, scientific description of a species helps to explain how it differs from similar species that have already been discovered and written about.

ECOSYSTEM

An ecosystem is a finely balanced environment, in which all the living things (plants, animals and other organisms) and non-living things (like rocks and the weather) work together to maintain the system's health.

ELECTRORECEPTION

Electroreception is an animal's ability to pick up on the electrical signals of another moving animal. It is mostly found in aquatic animals, as electricity travels better in water than in air. Electroreception can be used to find prey, avoid predators and find a mate.

ENDANGERED

An animal is considered endangered when there are so few of them that its species is at risk of becoming extinct and disappearing altogether.

EVOLUTION

Evolution is the process of gradual changes in organisms—humans, plants or animals—to help them adapt to their environment. Over long periods of time, environments change and creatures find new places to live, so animals and plants evolve to better suit their new conditions.

EXOSKELETON

An exoskeleton is the hard, shell-like covering around some animals, which functions to support and protect their body.

All insects and crustaceans have exoskeletons; their skeleton is on the outside of their body.

FILTER FEEDERS

A filter feeder is a type of aquatic animal that filters large amounts of sea water, usually through its very own specialized filtering system, to find enough food to eat. Some sharks are filter feeders.

FOSSIL

A fossil is the remains of a prehistoric animal or plant that are preserved inside a rock.

GENES

Genes are made of DNA, and they're the things that make each animal in the world unique. They exist inside the cells of living things, and are passed on from parents to their offspring. In humans, the combination of genes passed on by both parents can determine the appearance of the child, through things such as eye or hair color.

GENUS

A scientific name for a plant or animal is made up of a genus and a species name. A genus is a way to classify groups of animals or plants that have similar traits or features.

INVERTEBRATE

Invertebrates lack a backbone; they either have a gooey, spongy body (like jellyfish and worms) or they have an exoskeleton (like insects and crabs).

KRILL

Krill are tiny swimming crustaceans. They eat phytoplankton, a microscopic type of plankton that generally grows near the ocean's surface. Krill are the main food source for hundreds of different animals, including fish, whales and birds.

LARVAE

Many animals begin their lives as larvae before eventually growing into their adult form. Larvae generally look completely different from their parents, and often need very different conditions to survive. For example, tadpoles are the larvae of frogs.

MAMMALS

Mammals are a very broad class of animals. Some walk, some swim and some fly, and their diets can vary from carnivorous to herbivorous, but they all have a number of traits in common, including that they have hair or fur, feed their young with milk, and are warm-blooded.

METABOLISM

Metabolism refers to the chemical reactions that happen inside an organism to keep it alive. There are many different metabolic reactions, but the main ones involve releasing energy or using energy. For example, an animal's metabolism digests the food it eats and converts that food into a form that can be released as energy.

MIGRATION

Migration is a movement from one place to another. Animals often migrate each year at about the same time, and different species migrate for different reasons. Migrations commonly occur as animals travel to places where food is more plentiful, or to places where they can find a mate and breed.

ORGANISM

An organism is an animal, a plant or a single-celled life form.

PARASITE

A parasite is an organism that makes its home in or on an organism of another species, relying on it for food, shelter and everything else it needs to live. The organism that a parasite makes its home on is called its "host."

PLANKTON

Plankton are small living things—comprising both plants and animals—that drift along in the ocean and other bodies of water. Plankton is an essential food source for many animals, and certain types of plankton are also vital for releasing oxygen into the atmosphere.

POLLUTION

Pollution is the introduction of harmful materials or substances into our environment. The three main types of pollution are water, air and land pollution. One example of water pollution is microplastics in the ocean.

PREDATOR

In zoology, which is the scientific study of animals, the term "predator" usually refers to an animal that hunts other animals for food. Parasites are also a kind of predator. Predators are essential to a balanced ecosystem.

PREY

Prey is an animal that is hunted and killed by another animal for food.

ROV

ROV stands for Remotely Operated Vehicle. These robotic submarines are used by scientists for researching deep-sea creatures.

SCAVENGER

A scavenger is an animal that eats other animals that are already dead, rather than hunting for its own food.

SCUBA

SCUBA stands for Self-Contained Underwater Breathing Apparatus. Scuba divers use it so they can breathe underwater.

SEAMOUNTS

A seamount is an underwater island in a mountain range. Seamounts are usually formed by volcanoes.

SEDIMENT

Ocean sediment is tiny bits of rock and soil that drift through the water and settle on the sea floor.

SPECIES

A scientific name for a plant or animal is made up of a genus and a species name. A species is a group of similar organisms that are capable of breeding together.

SYMBIOSIS

Symbiosis is an interaction between two different plants or animals that live near each other—sometimes even on or inside each other—that benefits both of them.

TUBE FEET

Tube feet are fluid-filled tubes that stick out from an animal. They can be used for moving, eating, sensing or even breathing.

VERTEBRATE

Vertebrates are animals that have a spine and a well-developed skeleton inside their bodies.

PROFESSOR TiM FLANNERY

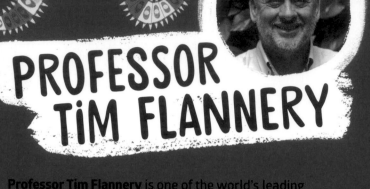

Professor Tim Flannery is one of the world's leading scientists, explorers, and conservationists. He's spent most of his life travelling the world to study different kinds of animals, and he's had some incredible adventures along the way—including digging up dinosaur bones, floating down crocodile-infested rivers, and wrestling pythons! He's discovered 75 brand-new species of animals—some that are still alive in the world today, and others that have been preserved as fossils. He's worked at museums and universities in Australia and around the world, and once even stayed at the American Museum of Natural History overnight! In 2007, he was named Australian of the Year. He's published more than 30 books for adults, as well as creating a number of documentaries. This is his second book for children, following *Weird, Wild, Amazing!*

SAM CALDWELL

Sam Caldwell loves drawing, especially pictures of animals. He grew up in the north of England, where he first discovered his passion for drawing, and now lives in Scotland, where he still spends most of his time drawing! Sam studied painting at the Edinburgh College of Art, and his illustrations have been featured in magazines, newspapers, and books in many corners of the world. You can see more of Sam's excellent animals illustrations in his first book with Tim Flannery: *Weird, Wild, Amazing!*

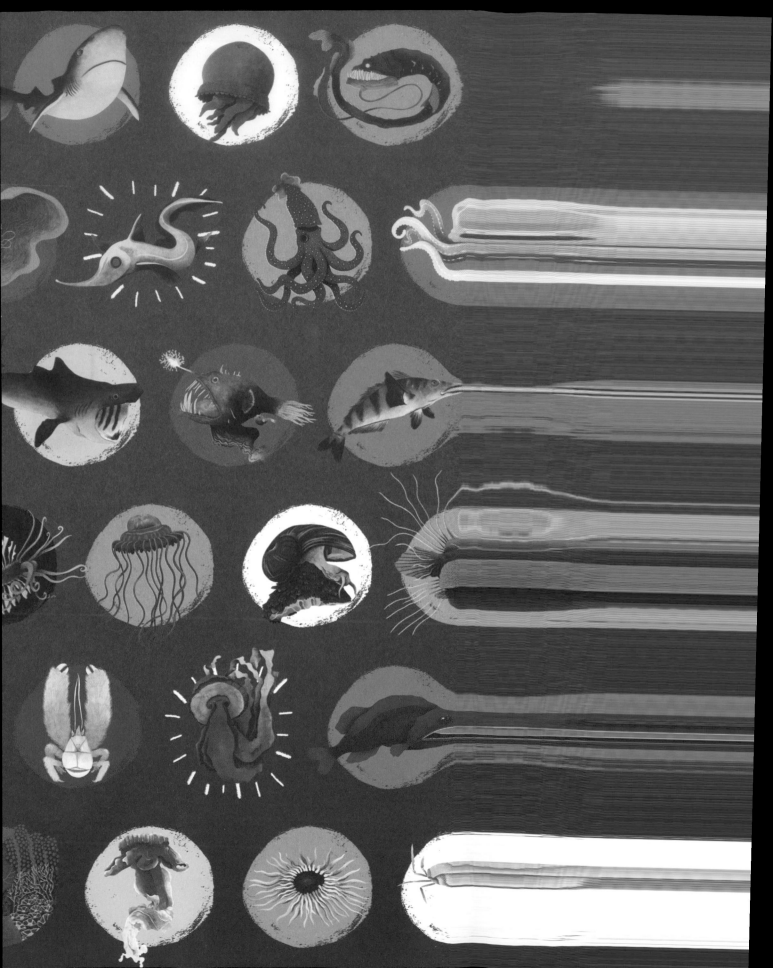